Aha! Moments

CONSUMER'S GUIDE TO THE HOLY SPIRIT

Jeffrey B. Thompson

WESTBOW
PRESS
A DIVISION OF THOMAS NELSON
& ZONDERVAN

Unless indicated otherwise, all scripture taken from THE HOLY BIBLE, NEW INTERNATIONAL VERSION®, NIV® Copyright © 1973, 1978, 1984, 2011 by Biblica, Inc.® Used by permission. All rights reserved worldwide.

Scripture marked KJV is taken from the King James Version of the Bible.

Cover image is from iStockphoto LP.

WestBow Press books may be ordered through booksellers or by contacting:

WestBow Press
A Division of Thomas Nelson & Zondervan
1663 Liberty Drive
Bloomington, IN 47403
www.westbowpress.com
1 (866) 928-1240

Because of the dynamic nature of the Internet, any web addresses or links contained in this book may have changed since publication and may no longer be valid. The views expressed in this work are solely those of the author and do not necessarily reflect the views of the publisher, and the publisher hereby disclaims any responsibility for them.

ISBN: 978-1-4908-3948-6 (sc)
ISBN: 978-1-4908-3949-3 (e)

Library of Congress Control Number: 2014910124

Printed in the United States of America.

WestBow Press rev. date: 06/13/2014

Contents

Introduction

Do you want to ignite a controversy? Attempt to explain the Third Person of the Trinity, the Holy Spirit. There are a multitude of divergent ideas suggested by serious scholars about how we relate to the Holy Spirit and what He is up to in this day and time. Even when the same words are used, the ideas often are quite diverse.

I have been a lawyer for 40 years before starting to write this book. Most of that time I was a trial lawyer. Communication was my stock in trade. I have been literally amazed at how differently people take the very same words. I learned relatively early in my legal career that what I felt I had clearly stated was not necessarily what was heard by the judge, opposing counsel and jury members.

For some time now, my wife Nancy and I have been teaching about our relationship with God and our participation in supernatural ministry. We start each series of discussions with the explanation of Baptism with the Holy Spirit contained in this book. After this explanation, we offer an opportunity for the class participants to ask (perhaps again) for a filling with the Holy Spirit. The participants experience greater clarity after this endeavor.

Ask Jesus to Baptize you with the Holy Spirit, afresh and anew, so that the Spirit of wisdom and revelation may bring you to a better knowledge of God – not a better knowledge of concepts and theology but rather to know God better.

The teachings in this book concerning the Holy Spirit are intended to emphasize and enhance each of our abilities to become aware of God's presence in our lives and participate in bringing God's compassion to His people on a consistent basis. Let us jointly search for and expect to find more and more avenues in which we experience God's presence and His power that always accompanies His presence. Apparently, He never leaves home without it. (My apologies to American Express.)

Nancy and I were transformed by the renewing of our minds in 2008. (See Romans 12:2) One of the benefits of a renewed mind is we can know the Holy Spirit differently. Nancy and I are now convinced that:

> A world in which God is not powerfully present and intimately involved in the lives of His people is a lie.

> A world in which the power of God is not demonstrated on a regular basis through miracles, signs and wonders is a lie.

> A world in which it is possible to pray in accordance with the will of God and nothing happens is a lie.

> A world in which God is not an active, loving participant is a lie.

> A world in which the Holy Spirit has withdrawn from active participation in the everyday life of believers is a lie.

We cannot expect to know and walk with the Holy Spirit if the world we perceive is a lie.

My purpose in this book is not to dogmatically establish a theology concerning our interaction with the Holy Spirit. Rather, my purpose is to present to you those aspects of the Holy Spirit which have become evident to us following our transformation.

Since 2008, we have experienced an explosion in the number of times we have been able to co-labor with God in bringing spiritual, emotional and physical healing to God's people. Our experience changed drastically when we changed the way we believed about kingdom matters.

I do not intend to suggest that what you have been taught and believed about the Holy Spirit and Baptism with the Holy Spirit is erroneous. I will leave those issues to theologians. Rather, my purpose is to present those aspects of the Holy Spirit that make more sense to us today now that we know Him better. When you know Him better, He will teach you what you should retain and what you should discard from your prior teaching.

If you are experiencing "answers to prayer" with a healing ratio in excess of 75%, feel free to disregard everything in this book that differs from from your doctrine. If, however, your prayers seem to be ineffectual much more often than you would like, feel free to adopt the concepts addressed in this book and see how your experience changes.

If you are a Type A personality, if you are accustomed to being one of the more capable individuals in your circle of acquaintances, if you have historically become better able to accomplish a task through practice and improved technique, I have disappointing news for you. In the context of supernatural ministry, there never comes a time when you get to do anything by yourself in your own power and gifting.

It has been a surprise to me that in this endeavor of co-laboring with God there seems to be no place for Jeffie to shine. Supernatural ministry always begins with Jesus, ends with Jesus and only Jesus occupies the middle ground. All kingdom activity is accomplished by manifestations of the Holy Spirit. Nothing is accomplished by manifestations of Jeffie. Bummer for me.

There is greater joy being a witness in the Holy Spirit's arena than being a star in my arena. Really, no comparison!

CHAPTER ONE

Get Over Yourself

B eing the "sharpest knife in the drawer" is often an advantage in gaining understanding. We are trained to look to and use our intellect in virtually all aspects of our lives. After all, the better I can understand a situation, the better equipped I am to discern the best solution to a problem, the truth of a situation and the path to select to overcome the problem.

Those who are used to being the sharpest knife in the drawer have become accustomed to having others look to them for explanations of the complicated aspects of life. I became a lawyer principally because I understood that I enjoyed being able to study a complicated issue and then relate that issue to others in an easily understood manner. I loved jury trials because the entire exercise involved communicating my client's position to people who were not familiar with the problem in a way that they would be able to gauge which version of the testimony was most likely the truth, most likely corresponded to the way the "world worked."

As a new Christian, I believed that a little study of the scriptures would reveal to me the truth with such clarity that I would be able to assist others in gaining the same understanding. It was somewhat baffling to learn that knowing with some specificity what the words were did not solve the puzzle. There was more at work than an intellectual understanding of the words used by the particular bible translators for the issue at hand.

Simply put, I believed that we come to believe in God by understanding Him and what He has said in His Word. Surely (I thought) we must rely on our intellect to learn the intricacies of God. Surely we need to understand the idea of an all-powerful, ever present, all-omniscient, eternal being.

What a shock to find that God did not agree with me! There were several troubling passages which seemed to reach out, grab me, and say, "Not so fast, Scooter."

What was I to make of Jesus telling us "unless you change and become like little children, you will never enter the kingdom of heaven"? (Matthew 18:3) It was bad enough that Matthew reported this statement but Luke also apparently heard the same thing. "Anyone who will not receive the kingdom of God like a little child will never enter it." (Luke 18:17)

The steps seem fairly clear. Step one is becoming like little children. Step two is receiving the kingdom as that little child you have become. Neither one of these steps requires that I be the sharpest knife in the drawer. In fact, being the sharpest knife in the drawer significantly interferes with our ability to become like little children. If we can succeed in becoming like little children, then there is the issue of receiving the kingdom while retaining your status as a little child. In other words, the little child's job is not to mature into the sharpest knife in the drawer. Receiving the kingdom of God is not assisted by an intellectual pursuit of understanding concepts and theologies.

The Apostle Paul talks about a veil which covers the hearts of the Israelites when the old covenant is read. According to Paul, this veil makes their minds dull. The veil can only be removed if Jesus takes it away. (2 Corinthians 3:14-15)

Then Paul explains, "[W]henever anyone turns to the Lord, the veil is taken away." (2 Corinthians 3:16) The veil is not removed through the acquisition of knowledge. The veil is removed when one turns to the Lord. Knowledge does not lead to belief. Belief leads to knowledge.

Paul did not ask the Ephesians to study the scriptures in order to become mature in their faith. Rather, he asked God to give them "the Spirit of Wisdom and Revelation so that [they] may know Him better." (Ephesians 1:17) Maturity for the Christian, according to Paul, was to be attained by knowing God, not by learning concepts.

It is my experience that the people in the pews are more than a little nervous about the Holy Spirit. For English speakers, the concept of the Holy Ghost carries with it some confusion. Just what is a ghost and how, if at all, is the Holy Ghost related to Casper the Friendly Ghost? Often this confusion about the Holy Ghost has made it quite convenient to accept some teachings from church leaders that suggest that the Holy Ghost is at least semi-retired. If He is active at all, He certainly is observing a reduced work schedule from biblical times. Unfortunately, nothing could be further from the truth.

In reading this book, I ask that you simply relax about what you have believed, what questions you have, and what doubts you have about the Holy Spirit. No matter what you believe, I promise you that there is a host of bible trained scholars who agree with you. You will able to find a multitude of teachings about the Holy Spirit to support virtually any position you have about Him.

So what can we do? Study harder? Read until we are thoroughly confused with intellectual explanations?

I suggest that the most reliable approach for non-theologians is to relax and rely upon a person with personal experience who we find to be reliable in reporting his or her observations.

Why do I not urge an exhaustive study of the scriptures and commentaries that in any manner mention the Holy Spirit? The answer is simple. God is too complex for us to understand. We tend to learn easily by a good analogy. Analogy is used to explain the unknown by likening that unknown idea to a known phenomenon. We see Jesus using analogy often. The kingdom of God is like a mustard seed. A mustard seed is the smallest of all seeds on earth. Yet, when it is planted, that mustard seed grows and becomes the largest of all garden plants. (Mark 4:30-32) We can visualize and understand the mustard seed, or at least some of its characteristics. The comparison of the kingdom to the mustard seed then sheds light on the kingdom. It is like the mustard seed. It is not a mustard seed, but it is **like** one.

There can be no satisfactory analogy for God. There is no equivalent which we may have experienced to which He can be compared. The Trinity cannot be analogized. Attempts such as "an egg is made of three parts, shell, yolk and white" are not analogous to Father, Son and Holy Spirit. A man may be a son, husband and father all at the same time but this reality is simply not the same as the relationship of the persons of the Trinity.

Remember, an intellectual understanding of God, whether of the Father, Son, Holy Spirit or all three, does not lead to faith. Rather, turning to the Lord is what removes the veil. Paul's promise is that "we all, who with unveiled faces contemplate the Lord's glory, are being transformed into His image with ever-increasing glory, which comes from the Lord, who is Spirit. (2 Corinthians 3:18) That's what we want, to be transformed into His image. Paul reminds us, "the Lord is the Spirit, and where the Spirit of the Lord is, there is freedom." (2 Corinthians 3:17)

In my undergraduate days at West Point, I was required to take a course in physics. I had not studied physics in high school and wondered what this would be about. I found that physics was, in large part, applied mathematics. Because I was good at math, I found I was good at physics. I simply accepted the principles of physics and applied the math principals I had already learned and physics was simple. I had no basis to accept or challenge the proposition that the measure of force would be equal to the mass of the object multiplied by the objects acceleration [$F=m \times a$]. If I accepted (like a child) that $F=m \times a$, I could excel in arriving at the correct solution. Physics was fun – until we got to electricity.

I don't understand electricity. When my professors could not explain whether the electrons which sprang out of the end of a wire under an electric current were those electrons from the beginning of the wire supplied by the electrical current traveling through the wire and then emerging or if those electrons were some other source, I was perplexed. The best understanding I have of electricity that I have to this day is that if you buy those plastic switches and outlets and put them on your wall, the hair dryer will work. Beyond that, ask someone else.

Although I have only an extremely elementary concept of electricity, I have felt the shock of putting my finger in the outlet. I have shorted out appliances trying to fix them with a knife down the toaster openings, etc. I know the truth of the power of electricity, the uses to which it can be put and the difference it makes to me to live in an electric powered environment. Because I have experienced the power of electricity and where to find it, I refuse to sit in the dark until I can understand all there is to know about electricity.

Knowledge of the power of the Holy Spirit, where to find Him, and the difference He makes in my life makes me, likewise, unwilling to sit in the kingdom without Him. I cannot afford to let what I don't know about the Holy Spirit rob me of what I have learned through turning in faith to have the veil removed. I am unwilling to settle for a life that does not include the power, wonder and amazement of co-laboring with the Holy Spirit. I am unwilling to settle for only so much of God as I can explain.

There are several things we know about the Holy Spirit which appear to trump all the questions that remain unanswered (or at least subject to considerable intellectual debate).

1. The Holy Spirit is God, Himself.
2. The Holy Spirit will never contradict either the Father or the Son.
3. Jesus promised to send the Holy Spirit when He departed from this earth.
4. The Holy Spirit inhabits each believer.

Why should you be concerned with the Holy Spirit? The Holy Spirit is essential for acceptance of the things of the kingdom. The Apostle John tells us "Yet to all who received him, to those who believed in his name, he gave the right to become children of God." (John 1:12) Receiving Jesus and believing in His name are essential to having the right to become children of God. That's how the veil is taken away.

One without the Holy Spirit is simply not equipped to understand the good news.

> [14] *After John was put in prison, Jesus went into Galilee, proclaiming the good news of God.*
> [15] *"The time has come," he said. "The kingdom of God has come near. Repent and believe the good news!"* (Mark 1:14-15)

Metanoio, the Greek word translated "repent" in that scripture means to change your way of **thinking**. Your way of thinking cannot be changed if you are not equipped to spiritually discern the truths of the gospel.

Paul tells us,

> *The man without the Spirit does not accept the things that come from the Spirit of God, for they are foolishness to him, and he cannot understand them, because they are spiritually discerned.* (1 Corinthinans 2:14)

It is critical to one's efforts to co-labor with God to have the Holy Spirit equipping him to spiritually discern those things that, absent the Holy Spirit, can only be considered foolishness.

It is important to note that Paul does not say that the man without **intellectual understanding** of the Spirit does not accept the things that come from the Spirit. Rather, the requirement for spiritual discernment is to have the Holy Spirit.

CHAPTER TWO

Co-Laboring
Who's on First?

I n all things, God is in charge and we are not. That is really
good news!

There is considerable confusion about the Holy Spirit's
role and our role in supernatural ministry. A lot of the confusion
can be traced to our limited understanding of the "gifts of the
Holy Spirit."[1] Does the Holy Spirit impart gifts or abilities to us
that become personal to us? Can we "do the stuff" under our
own power? What is this "power from on high"? What part do
we play? Who's on first?

The most attractive analogy for me is the trolley cars in cities
like San Francisco in days gone by. The trolley cars became electric
powered (after some time of horse drawn cars). While powered by
electricity, the trolley ran on rails which established the path of
travel. The rails ran underneath overhead power lines to which
the trolley car was attached.

---

[1] See Chapters Seven and Nine for discussion of these matters.

The trolley cars did not have giant batteries or reservoirs of power on board. The required power could not be contained in an on-board battery because the power required to "do the job" outstripped the capacity of any battery.

The attachment to the overhead power lines connected the motor to the source of the power. The motor was not an engine capable of producing power on its own by consumption of fuel like our gasoline engines. Rather, all the power for the motor came from a source outside the trolley car.

The need for power confined the trolley cars to the designated route. Leaving the track carried with it a break from the source of the power for movement. The trolley car could perform all of its intended functions if connected to the source but none of its intended functions when detached.

So it is with the Holy Spirit. The power of the Holy Spirit resides in the Holy Spirit, not in us. (Admittedly, the Holy Spirit resides in us.) Should we deviate from the designated course, we become separated from the power and find ourselves quite unable to "do the stuff." The intimate relationship we have with the Holy Spirit is entirely necessary for anything to be accomplished in the kingdom. If we can do it without the Holy Spirit, it is not a ministry.

Just as the trolley car motor is a co-laborer with the electrical source, we participate in miracles, signs and wonders as a fellow worker with God. The concept of "God's fellow workers" or "workers together with God" (2 Corinthians 6:1) contains an important relational truth. Make no mistake; He always has the laboring oar. God is the worker; we are the fellow workers. We work together with God. He doesn't work together with us. We have the privilege of working together with God. He does not help us (as we so often like to pray) but rather lets us witness his majesty, power and glory while "assisting" Him.

The issue of power is addressed directly in Acts. After the beggar and Peter and John met at the temple gate called Beautiful and was completely healed, Peter said to the gathered crowd:

> *Why do you stare at us as if by our own power or holiness we had made this man walk? . . . It is Jesus' name and the faith that comes through him that has completely healed him, as you can all see."* (Acts: 3:12, 16)

Annas, the high priest, Caiaphas and other rulers, elders and teachers of the law had Peter and John brought before them and questioned them.

> *"By what power or what name did you do this?" . . .*

> *Then, Peter, filled with the Holy Spirit said to them, . . . "It is by the name of Jesus Christ of Nazareth whom you crucified but whom God raised from the dead, that this man stands before you healed."* (Acts 4:7-10)

Surely if the power imparted at Pentecost deposited a personal ability or power in the recipients, Peter and John would have received that power. However, they specifically deny any power or holiness residing in them to heal this beggar.

My wife, Nancy, and I began to participate in miracles, signs and wonders when we stopped asking God to bless what we were doing. We don't ask God to help us to accomplish our agenda. Rather, we seek to determine what God is already blessing and participate in that. It is His agenda, not ours. The concept of dying to self includes abandoning our agenda and fully embracing His agenda. His agenda is always better, not to mention more fun.

Jesus did not come to us to receive His rest. We come to Jesus to receive our rest. He does not take our yoke upon Him. We take His yoke upon us. When we remember who is on first we are properly yoked.

> *"Take my yoke upon you and learn from me, for I am gentle and humble in heart, and you will find rest for your souls. For my yoke is easy and my burden is light."* (Matthew 11:29-30)

Now, that's the way I want to work. What could be better than to be coupled with a much stronger partner who is both gentle and humble and who will let me rest? If I am going to be yoked, I need that yoke to be easy.

Bad News for Type A Personalities

Another part of getting over yourself is accepting the subservient role in "doing the stuff." As a type-A personality, I long for opportunities to be in charge, in control, and have the most important task coupled with substantial ability. That's what seemed to be fulfilling before being yoked with Jesus and watching Him work.

As I write this, Nancy and I are completing our sixth year of co-laboring with God in supernatural ministry. I have yearned for the time when the coach would send me to the plate to try for that home run. In the last six years, I have come to realize that I don't ever get a time at bat. Jesus is always at the plate now and "on deck" at the same time. He is not selfish about who will advance the ball. He knows that the team relies upon having the best, most capable batter at the plate and the fastest runner on base at all times. The outcome of the game is too important to settle for a less capable substitute for the King of Kings and Lord of Lords.[2]

A Matter of Positioning

God is so far ahead of us it is staggering. The occurrences we find so convenient and amazing God has had planned for eons. The set-up for the miraculous things of today was prepared long ago. He is the one who brings both parties to the table, the person praying and the one receiving prayer. He brings those parties together at just the right time for Him to pour out His compassion on His people. God is an expert at positioning us so that we may participate in His miraculous interventions in history.

The Aramean siege of the nation of Israel in the walled city of Samaria illustrates clearly how God acts through His people in supernatural ways to accomplish His purposes. It is crystal clear that no one intentionally did anything to accomplish the miracle described yet God blessed all of His people.

Let's identify the players.

The Government.

Joram, a son of Ahab, became king of Israel in the northern kingdom, which consisted of ten tribes. Joram's capital city was the walled city of Samaria. He got rid of the "sacred stone of Baal" which Ahab had made but he clung to the sins of Jeroboam. (2 Kings 3:1-2)

---

[2] See Chapter Nine for a discussion of the power from on high and what it means to be Jesus' witnesses.

The Church.

Elisha was a significant prophet. He had no use for Joram whatsoever. (2 Kings 3:14) Elisha had a prior history of participating in miracles. He had raised the Shunnamite's son from the dead. (2 Kings 4:31-36) He was involved in Naaman's healing from leprosy. (2 Kings 5:1-15)

The Enemy.

Naaman was the commander of the Aramean army. He was healed of his leprosy when he reluctantly followed Elisha's instructions to dip himself in the Jordan seven times.

Ben Haddad was the king of Aram. He had continuing controversies with Joram and the nation of Israel. He had previously sent some of his army to capture Elisha but failed completely.

God was teaching Israel that its security came from Him alone, not from Joram (the government) and not from Elisha (the church). In the midst of those circumstances, Ben Haddad sent his entire army, commanded by Naaman, to lay siege to the walled city of Samaria. The siege caused a severe famine within the city. The famine was so bad that two women made a pact to kill and eat their babies. After the first baby was eaten, the second mother reneged and hid her child.

Joram received the complaint of the second woman while he was walking the walls of the city. His immediate response was anger toward Elisha, apparently believing this bad fortune for the nation of Israel was part of the on-going battle between the two.

In the midst of the famine and hidden baby problem, Elisha prophesied:

> *"Hear the word of the LORD. This is what the LORD says: About this time tomorrow, a seah of flour will sell for a shekel and two seahs of barley for a shekel at the gate of Samaria."* (2 Kings 7:1)"

This prophecy was met with complete skepticism.

Sitting outside the walled city of Samaria were four lepers who were considered unclean and were completely unwelcome in the city. The only thing the lepers shared with the Nation of Israel was the famine.

The same day that Elisha prophesied the coming abundance of food, the lepers had an interesting conversation.

> *"Why sit we here until we die? If we say, 'We will enter into the city,' then the famine is in the city, and we shall die there; and if we sit still here, we die also. Now therefore come, and let us fall unto the host of the Syrians; if they save us alive, we shall live; and if they kill us, we shall but die."* (2 Kings 7:3-4 KJV)

"Why sit we here until we die?" This is a critical question for all believers. Once I am saved, what am I to do? Is there a purpose for me or do I just sit here until I die?

The lepers decided on that occasion, not a day before or day later, to go to the enemy's camp. While they were on the way, and totally unbeknownst to them, God performed a miracle that rescued the entire nation of Israel.

> *"The Lord . . . caused the Arameans to hear the sound of chariots and horses and a great army, so that they said to one another, "Look, the king of Israel has hired the Hittite and Egyptian kings to attack us!" So they got up and fled in the dusk and abandoned their tents and their horses and donkeys. They left the camp as it was and ran for their lives."*
> (2 Kings 7:6-7)

The food and provisions that the army left behind saved the lives of the entire nation of Israel.

Consider these questions and then decide who is on first.

- Who performed the miracle?
- Who participated in the miracle?
- What part did each play?
- Who got the glory?

God alone caused the Aramean army to hear chariots and horses and a great army. The Aramean army did not flee for fear of the approaching lepers. They were terrified by what God caused them to hear.

Neither the lepers nor any of the residents of the walled city of Samaria heard those chariots and horses. The reason is simple — the army did not exist in the physical realm!

The church didn't do it.

Elisha cannot be credited for the miracle. Elisha did nothing except repeat what he heard God saying. He did absolutely nothing to bring this result to pass. He did not call the nation of

Israel to prayer or take any action. God said it and Elisha repeated what he had heard God say.

The government didn't do it.

Joram cannot be credited for the miracle. Joram did nothing except threaten to kill Elisha. He did not even call out to God for help.

The enemy didn't do it.

Naaman cannot be credited for the miracle. Naaman stood in awe of the God of Israel because he had experienced the power of God when God healed him from leprosy.

Naaman knew that his army was laying siege to a nation that was blessed by God Himself. When Naaman and his soldiers heard the sound of horses and chariots, he believed that other nation's armies were coming. The Aramean army ran in fear.

The lepers didn't do it.

The lepers cannot be credited for the miracle. The enemy did not depart in fear of the approaching lepers. The enemy was terrified by sounds of a heavenly host that only they could hear. The lepers had no expectation that the Aramean army would hear the sound of horses and chariots and flee.

The lepers' function in the miracle was to report the good news and share the bounty. God prompted the four lepers to get up at that very moment. They had no knowledge of Elisha's prophesy of abundance. Had they not gone, when would the nation of Israel have learned that God was blessing them with abundance? All the lepers knew was they were walking to the

Aramean camp either for food or for death. They had no intention of participating in a miracle.

There was activity all around. However, God is the one who performed the miracle. All the others were positioned to report the good news of God's miraculous intervention on behalf of His people.

God did not perform this miracle because of:

- Elisha's actions as a prophet;
- Joram's actions as king of Israel;
- a desire to punish Naaman or Ben Haddad;
- any "righteousness" of the lepers; or
- the goodness of anyone in the circumstance.

God performed this miracle for the same reason He performs them all – because He is good and He loves His people.

He was not rewarding anyone for good actions. The people of Israel were killing and eating their children. The government was at odds with the church. Distrust and destructive behavior was rampant. They weren't good. He was.

No one realized God was performing a miraculous intervention in Israel's history and pouring out His compassion on His people while it was happening. The realization of the truth awaited a report from the unclean and unwelcome lepers of the blessings now available to God's people.

No one did anything more than be where God positioned them and report what he saw and heard. The religious followers of Elisha (and Elisha himself) were unable to deliver God's compassion to His people. The existing government, Joram and his army could do nothing other than permit the blessing to be received. Most likely, the ones who reported the blessing were still not permitted within the city because the leprosy persisted.

God did it all, from beginning to end. He intervened in the history of His people to demonstrate His compassion and His love. No one prayed to God to change His mind. God was not rewarding the faith of anyone involved in the circumstances.

Each of the lepers was a fellow worker with God. He didn't help them perform the miracle. The miracle was not a product of power He granted to them. Rather, He positioned them in a way to observe and report what He was doing.

Elisha was a fellow worker with God. God didn't help Elisha accomplish any result. Elisha was positioned in a way to speak God's word to the people so that when the miracle was discovered the following day all the glory would be given to God.

All the co-laboring followed God's plan, not man's plan. What could be easier than simply being in the right place, positioned by God, and doing what God prompts you to do when He prompts you to do it? Had the lepers jumped the gun, they likely would have been killed. Instead, God prompted them to take their halting steps **on that day** in pursuit of His purposes.

The lepers were not experts in delivering God's compassion to His people. Yet, they were used mightily by God to accomplish His purposes.

Miraculous healings today are accomplished in exactly the same fashion. Someone may have a word of knowledge that God is going to heal a particular person or a particular condition. However, that knowledge does not enable the person in his own power to heal anyone. The person being healed may feel something and recognize the power of God is upon him, or he may not. The confirmation of many miraculous healings awaits a sensory perception of a change that cannot be explained in any way other than an act of God.

God had lots of witnesses to His power, majesty and glory. However, no one else went to the plate to try to hit one out of the park.

CHAPTER THREE

How Did Jesus Do That?

T he power of the Holy Spirit is what Jesus relied upon in each report of his healings and miracles. Although Jesus is now and always has been God Himself (John 1:1), while He walked the earth as a man He could not heal the sick, raise the dead or cast out demons by his own power. Jesus did not perform the miracles He participated in because He was divine. He participated in each of those circumstances as a man in right relation to His Father.

If you insist that Jesus was able to perform miracles, signs and wonders because He is God, you will likely find it difficult to believe His promise that "anyone who has faith in me will do what I have been doing." (John 14:12) You will look for an out. You will search for a definition of "anyone" that does not include you. You will find it very hard to take Jesus at His word.

If, however, you are willing to accept that Jesus operated on earth under self-imposed limitations, the possibilities for our participation with God in miracles, signs and wonders through the power of the Holy Spirit become limitless. These limitless possibilities bring with them a charge and responsibility to act in the kingdom as you have been authorized to act.

Self Imposed Limitations

While Jesus walked the earth as a man, He set aside most of His prerogatives by self imposed limitations.

"Like what?" you ask. God is omnipresent; He is everywhere. While walking this earth, Jesus was not omnipresent. He was not physically present in Samaria at the same time He was physically present in Jerusalem.

God is omniscient or all knowing. While He was here, Jesus was not. Someone who is all knowing cannot be surprised. Jesus was not only surprised, He was astonished. (Matthew 8:10) Someone who is omniscient already knows all things and cannot learn new things. However, Jesus learned about the condition of the invalid beside the pool of Bethesda. (John 5:6)

"Wait," you say. We are not in the same situation as Jesus. Surely He was able to heal everyone who came to Him because He was God. Since we are not God, we cannot expect to be able to heal anyone. That is solely God's province. The proper response to this argument is "Yes" and "No."

The "Yes": It has always been and always will be the province of God to provide the power to heal and deliver from torment.

The "No": Jesus, the man, had no power to heal. He could not raise the dead. He could not deliver from torment. He could not cast out demons. With His self-imposed limitations He stood before the Father as we do.

Nonetheless, Jesus was God. He was the exact representation of the Father. (Hebrews 1:3) All the fullness of God Himself lived in Jesus. (1 Colossians 2:9) Yet, Jesus was made like us in every way. (Hebrews 2:17)

Since Jesus is God, how can I say that Jesus had no power to heal, could not raise the dead, deliver from torment or cast out demons under his own power? I say that Because He Said So.

After healing the invalid by the pool of Bethesda, (John, Chapter 5) Jesus was questioned about healing on the Sabbath. (Don't religious leaders amaze you? Forget the fact that the invalid was healed. Let's be religious and question the day of the week rather than be astounded at the power of God.)

Jesus gave them this answer:

> *"I tell you the truth, the Son can do nothing by Himself; he can do only what he sees his Father doing, because whatever the Father does the Son also does."* (John 5:19)

This statement deals directly with power and authority, not choice or volition. Jesus didn't say He chose not to do anything unless He saw the Father doing it. He said He **could not** do anything by Himself.

If I take Jesus at His word, Jesus had no power to do anything by Himself. While He walked the earth, Jesus was completely dependent upon the power of the Holy Spirit.

Jesus Modeled Behavior

Jesus' actions were not principally designed to illustrate the power of God. God's power was recorded and well recognized throughout the Old Testament. Jesus did not need to do one thing to illustrate that God was able to do all He needed to do to accomplish His purposes.

Jesus' actions modeled the power made available to a man standing in right relation to God. If the same right relation to God is available to us, we have a perfect model of what we can expect to accomplish in the kingdom.

How Did Jesus Pray?

How do you suppose Jesus prayed? What guidance and direction did He seek from the Father? Because He was not omnipresent, Jesus had to rely on the Father to position Him where God was going to act and direct Him what to do. I believe that a lot of Jesus' prayer time was dedicated to discovering where God was directing Him to go next and who the focus of God's attention in that place would be.

We can pray for the exact same guidance and direction. Although God is omnipresent, He is not acting through us throughout the world. Rather, His action through us necessarily occurs where we are. Just like Jesus, we need to understand where we need to be and who the objects of God's compassion are before we will be able to participate as co-laborers with God in any situation.

Baptism by John

Every miracle, sign and wonder performed by Jesus followed His baptism by John. When He came out of the water, scripture records the Spirit of God descended upon him like a dove and remained. (John 1:33)

Peter explained the source of Jesus' power this way:

You know *"what has happened throughout Judea, beginning in Galilee after the baptism that John preached —how God anointed Jesus of Nazareth with the Holy Spirit and power, and how he went around doing good and healing all who were under the power of the devil, because God was with him."* (Acts 10:37-38)

Jesus relied upon the Holy Spirit for all the power He needed to accomplish what the Father desired. We have access to the very same power. Peter finishes with the reminder that Jesus did all He did because God was with him. If the Holy Spirit was not present to act, Jesus got nothing done. The Holy Spirit was the source of the power to do those things the Father was doing. When Jesus testified that He could only do what He saw the Father doing He was admitting that unless the Father had sent the Holy Spirit to perform miracles, signs and wonders, there would be no miracles, signs and wonders. It is God who performed the miracles, signs and wonders through the power of the Holy Spirit, not Jesus the man.

> On the day of Pentecost, Peter said: *"Jesus of Nazareth was a man accredited by God to you by miracles, wonders and signs, which God did among you through him, as you yourselves know."* (Acts 2:22)

Jesus did not perform the miracles, wonders and signs. Rather, God performed the miracles, wonders and signs by acting through Jesus. God was the actor, not Jesus. Jesus was the perfect vessel. Jesus was a perfect host for the presence of God. The Spirit remained on Him.

Luke, the author of both the Gospel of Luke and the Book of the Acts of the Apostles, was a physician. With his medical background, Luke is likely a trustworthy reporter of the nature of the healings he described. Luke recounts the healing of an invalid lowered through a roof on his bed to be placed in front of Jesus.

One day as he was teaching, Pharisees and teachers of
the law, who had come from every village of Galilee
and from Judea and Jerusalem, were sitting there.
And the power of the Lord was present for him to
heal the sick. (Luke 5:17)

Luke knew that by Himself Jesus could do nothing. How did he know? Jesus told him (and us)! Luke also knew that when Jesus saw what the Father was doing, all things were possible. Thus, Luke records that the power of the Lord was present for him to heal the sick. Absent this power, nothing would have happened. How do I know that? Because He Said So.

Not only was Jesus able to do only what He saw the Father doing, He was very careful about his tongue. Jesus only said what He heard the Father saying. Jesus said, "I do nothing on my own but speak just what the Father has taught me." (John 5:28)

Jesus did not claim to speak of His own authority. He claimed that the Father commanded Him not only what to say but also how to say it. (John 12:49)

Jesus was not guarding His tongue to avoid sinning by His words. He guarded His tongue because He recognized that His words had extraordinary power. Jesus said, "The words I have spoken to you are spirit and they are life." (John 6:63) Peter confessed that Jesus had "the words of eternal life." (John 6:67) If Jesus spoke it, it came to pass. It came to pass because Jesus only said what He heard the Father saying in the manner the Father told Him to say it.

Isn't that the very definition of prophecy? Prophecy is saying the words of God in the manner God has instructed.

We can discern an important truth from this discussion of Jesus' care to say only what the Father was saying. Many teachers today claim that the tongue is so powerful that we can speak things into existence by the power of our declaration. Thus, we see many Christians declaring the things they wish to see happen and wondering why the things they have declared have not occurred.

We do have power in our tongue through our declaration. However, since it is always God who is at bat, unless God has already declared what we are saying, our declaration has little efficacy, if any. It is God and God alone who can call things that are not as if they were.

The Power of Prophecy

God's word, once spoken, has power to accomplish God's purposes. God spoke the world into existence. God's word has incredible power and does not return to Him void.

> *"My word that goes out from my mouth . . . will not return to me empty, but will accomplish what I desire and achieve the purpose for which I sent it."* (Isaiah 55:11)

If God didn't say it, it isn't prophecy. It may be an accurate prediction of the future but it is not prophecy unless God says it.

A prophet is only a spokesman, not an interpreter. Spokesmen, by definition, speak for others, not themselves. Spokesmen give utterance to words, ideas and concepts that have no reality unless authorized by the person sending the spokesman. Spokesmen have no power to bring their words to pass unless the one for whom they speak has that power.

CHAPTER FOUR

Who Is The Holy Spirit?

D o you want to participate in supernatural ministry? Is it your desire to co-labor with God Himself in bringing His compassion to His people? Do miracles, signs and wonders hold an allure for you that won't go away? If so, your goal should be to know God better.

Participation in supernatural ministry is not the result of learning new concepts. It is not the result of memorizing "healing scriptures." What is required is a better knowledge of God. The goal is to know Him. Just believing in the idea of God is not enough.

Part of knowing God better is to get thoroughly acquainted with the Holy Spirit. You will find He is quite a guy. The more miracles you witness and participate in, the more you will become convinced of God's goodness and love for us. The longer you spend in God's presence, the easier it becomes to understand that He does it all while we simply witness His majesty and glory.

I assume that the readers of this book are familiar with the doctrine of the Trinity and recognize the Holy Spirit as the third person of the Godhead. However, since the concept of the Trinity can scarcely be understood, much less explained, to our rational minds, the Spirit of Wisdom and Revelation is completely necessary to help us accept without understanding that God is described and acts in three persons, Father, Son and Holy Spirit.

Since Jesus, God the Son, was a historical person, we are prone to accept Him. He is the only one of the Trinity anyone has seen "with skin on."

The Holy Spirit, on the other hand, in my formative years, was referred to as the Holy Ghost. I am of an age that my awareness of the idea of a Holy Ghost corresponded with the popularity of Casper the Friendly Ghost in the comic books and in cartoons on TV. This association in my mind was not helpful in any understanding of the Holy Ghost as a person and part of the Trinity.

Many Christians today have had precious little teaching about the Holy Spirit other than a quick reference as the third member of the Trinity. He makes many clergy and most in the pews nervous. So, let's take a few minutes and discuss who He is – not **what** He is, but **who**.

According to the Nicene Creed, the Holy Spirit is the Lord and Giver of Life. He proceeds from the Father and the Son. With the Father and Son He is worshipped and glorified. He spoke by the prophets. Everyone clear now? No? No wonder.

If the Holy Spirit is Lord, and the Father is described as Lord and Jesus is Lord, it is a pretty good bet that each better all be God. And they are!

"Lordship" is properly ascribed to each and every person of the Godhead. Indeed, any attempt to remove "lordship" from the Father, Son or Holy Spirit leads to nothing but confusion and misunderstanding. How can all be Lord at the same time? They just are! After all, they are only one God. How could one be Lord and another lack that attribute?

If you ask the Father whether the Holy Spirit is Lord, His answer will be, "Of course." Conversely, if you ask the Holy Spirit if the Father is Lord, His answer will be "Certainly, why do you ask?"

Maybe Giver of Life will be easier. Not so fast, Scooter. There is no spiritual life without God. God breathed his life into Adam. What part of God's presence gives spiritual life is complicated to express with precision.

Jesus said, *"whoever hears my word and believes him who sent me has eternal life and will not be condemned but has crossed over from death to life."* (John 5:24) Hearing and believing brings this change from death to life, but who does it?

The Father raises the dead and gives them life. (John 5:21) The Son gives life to whom he is pleased to give it. (John 5:21) The Holy Spirit gives us life by residing in us.

Another Paraclete

Jesus said, *"I will ask the Father and he will give you **another Advocate** to help you and be with you forever, the Spirit of truth."* (John 14:16-18)

In John 14:16 the Greek word translated "another" is *allos*. A different Greek word which can be translated "another" is *heteros*, but that is not the word used here.

The essential difference between *allos* and *heteros* is that *allos* means another of the same kind, character and same everything to the first while *heteros* refers to another which is different from the first.

The same or a different what? Some translations speak of another Comforter rather than another Advocate. Both are correct. The Greek word translated as Comforter or Advocate is *parakletos*. A paraclete is, literally, one summoned to stand beside. The assistance and function of the paraclete depends upon the needs of the moment. Thus, a paraclete may be either a Comforter or an Advocate, depending upon the situation. In all situations, however, the paraclete is one who is summoned.

Baptism with the Holy Spirit is available to *all who ask.* (Matthew 7:11; Luke 11:17) The requirement to ask emphasizes the idea of "one who is summoned." Unless the Holy Spirit is summoned, that is, requested, there will be no Baptism with the Holy Spirit. Only Jesus baptizes with the Holy Spirit and He baptizes only those who ask.

Back to *allos.* Jesus said He would ask the Father to send another, identical paraclete. Identical to whom? Jesus is preparing his disciples for his departure. In this context He assures them they will not be left alone but will have Him present with them at all times in the form of "*allos parakletos.*" Jesus promised His presence through the presence of the Holy Spirit. The Holy Spirit is identical to Jesus without skin on.

One internet writer has expressed John 14:16-17 in this way:

> "I will pray the Father, and He will send you Someone who is just like Me in every way. He will be identical to Me in the way He speaks, the way He thinks, the way He operates, the way He sees things, and the way He does things. He will be exactly like Me in every way. If the Holy Spirit is here, it will be just as if I am here because we think, behave, and operate exactly the same."

Now that's good news!

Indeed, the word *parakletos* is also used to describe Jesus before the Father. (See 1 John 2:1) Both Jesus and the Holy Spirit are the *Parakletos*, and properly so because they are one and the same. In each instance of the use of *parakletos*, the gospel writer is John, the Beloved Apostle. John was not confused about the identity of Jesus and the Holy Spirit; he knew and experienced them both.

The word "paraclete" has been defined to include comforter, intercessor, advocate, consoler, encourager, uplifter, refresher, and teacher. *Parakletos* as used in the Gospel of John to describe the Holy Spirit is not specific as to the function of the one called alongside. The various translations of this Greek word into English is illustrative of the theology of the translator. You may feel the context leans one direction or another but the word is always the same, *parakletos*. The *Paraclete* has many functions and many descriptions but He is always called alongside by specific request in a particular circumstance. The all-powerful Holy Spirit can and does perform each of the functions of the *Paraclete* as He delivers Gods compassion to His people.

Jesus promised that we would know the Holy Spirit because He lives with us and will be in us. (John 14:17) This completes God's promise in both the Old and New Testament that God will never leave you nor forsake you. (See Deuteronomy 31:6; 31:8; Joshua 1:5; 1 Kings 8:57; Hebrews 13:5)

There are some inescapable conclusions which flow from the fact that the Holy Spirit is God Himself and is identical in every way to Jesus, The first conclusion is that there will never be a conflict between the will of the Holy Spirit, Jesus or the Father. Just as Jesus and the Father did not disagree, the Holy Spirit will never disagree with the Father.

The Holy Spirit reveals the Father. Jesus was an exact representation of the Father's being. (Hebrews 1:3) Since the Holy Spirit speaks, thinks and operates the same way Jesus did/does, the Holy Spirit is likewise an exact representation of the Father.

The absence of any conflict among the three persons of the Trinity should be obvious when we recall there is but one God who manifests Himself in three persons. There is no confusion in the mind of God. God does not think one way about one issue in His Father side of His mind and yet another way about that same issue in His Holy Spirit side of His mind.

Jesus was made manifest to destroy the works of the devil. (1 John 3:8) After Jesus of Nazareth was anointed by God with the Holy Spirit and with power, He went around doing good, healing all who were under the oppression of the devil, because God was with Him. (Acts 10:38) The Holy Spirit, being like Jesus in every way, can be relied upon to perform in exactly the same way today. He is still in the business of enforcing and demonstrating the destruction of the works of the devil, a finished work.

He still anoints Christians with power from on high so that they may go around healing all who are under the oppression of the devil. Just like Jesus, those Christians similarly anointed by the Holy Spirit and with power will only be able to do those things Jesus was doing because God is with us. He is with us in the form of the Holy Spirit.

Jesus went around doing good. Scripture does not report that Jesus went around being good, although that is undoubtedly true. The emphasis of this verse is what Jesus was accomplishing. He was "doing good." In the Greek language, emphasis is sometimes added by repetition. We see repetition in the Greek in Acts 10:38. The Greek says that Jesus "went around/went around doing good/ doing good."

Peter made sure that Cornelius and his whole household understood that Jesus sought out the people (He didn't wait for them to come to Him for an office visit) and then acted.

The Greek word translated "doing good" in this verse means "to be philanthropic." Jesus went out among the people and gave away all He had. What He had was the power of the Holy Spirit resting on Him from the time of His baptism by John. John saw the Holy Spirit descend upon Jesus in the form of a dove, **and remain**. (John 1:33)

Jesus made sure He only did what He saw the Father doing and said only what the Father said, in the way He was supposed to say it. (John 5:19, 30; John 8:28; John 12:49) Indeed Jesus confessed that he was **unable** to do anything other that what He saw the Father do. (John 5:19) Jesus knew that an important element in hosting the presence of the Holy Spirit upon Him was to adhere to the Father's plan, both in word and in action. The total identity between Jesus and the Holy Spirit means that the Holy Spirit will only do what He sees the Father doing and only say what He hears the Father saying.

The identity between Jesus and the Holy Spirit clarifies for us the will of the Holy Spirit. The Holy Spirit is still in the business of healing all who are afflicted by the devil. He is likewise intent on giving away every blessing to God's people (and will seek them out in order to do that).

CHAPTER FIVE

What the Bible Says About Baptism with the Holy Spirit

T he Bible is quite clear about those aspects of Baptism with the Holy Spirit that are addressed. Unfortunately, the specifics are sparse. This sparseness of the scriptures has led to many different "divinely inspired guesses" about Baptism with the Holy Spirit. So, what is it the Bible says on this subject?

John the Baptist

John the Baptist's primary function was to identify and prepare the way for the Messiah. In speaking about the Messiah he variously said:

> "*He will baptize you with the Holy Spirit and with fire.* (Matthew 3:11)

> "*I baptize with water, but He will baptize you with the Holy Spirit.*" (Mark 1:8)

> *"I baptize you with water. But . . . He will baptize*
> *you with the Holy Spirit and with fire."* (Luke 3:16)

In each instance, John was referring to one is "more powerful than I" and "the straps of whose sandals I am not worthy to untie." (Luke 3:16) Identification awaits the Gospel of John:

> *"The next day John saw Jesus coming toward him*
> *and said, 'Look, the Lamb of God, who takes away*
> *the sin of the world! This is the one I meant when I*
> *said, 'A man who comes after me has surpassed me*
> *because he was before me.' I myself did not know*
> *him, but the reason I came baptizing with water*
> *was that he might be revealed to Israel.*
>
> *Then John gave this testimony: 'I saw the Spirit come*
> *down from heaven as a dove and remain on him.*
> *And I myself did not know him, but the one who*
> *sent me to baptize with water told me, 'The man*
> *on whom you see the Spirit come down and remain*
> *is the one who will baptize with the Holy Spirit.' I*
> *have seen and testify that this is God's Chosen One."*
> (John 1:29-34)

The scripture nowhere identifies anyone other than Jesus who is able to baptize with the Holy Spirit. Although each of us may baptize with water, none of us has a scriptural basis to baptize with the Holy Spirit. Prayers for Baptism with the Holy Spirit should, therefore, be addressed to Jesus.

In a somewhat enigmatic statement, John says that he came baptizing with water so that "he" might be revealed to Israel. One explanation for that statement is that John was sent to preach a baptism of repentance for the forgiveness of sins. (Luke 3: 3) During Jesus' baptism, God revealed His Chosen One by the descent of the Holy Spirit who then remained on Him.

Jesus

Jesus made specific reference to Baptism with the Holy Spirit. On resurrection Sunday, Jesus held a team meeting with the Apostles.

> [36] *While they were still talking about this, Jesus himself stood among them and said to them, "Peace be with you."*
> [37] *They were startled and frightened, thinking they saw a ghost.*

> [44] *He said to them, "This is what I told you while I was still with you: Everything must be fulfilled that is written about me in the Law of Moses, the Prophets and the Psalms."*
> [45] *Then he opened their minds so they could understand the Scriptures.*
> [46] *He told them, "This is what is written: The Messiah will suffer and rise from the dead on the third day,*
> [47] *and repentance for the forgiveness of sins will be preached in his name to all nations, beginning at Jerusalem.*
> [48] *You are witnesses of these things.*
> [49] *I am going to send you what my Father has promised; but stay in the city until you have been clothed with power from on high." (Luke 24:36-49)*

There are several important "take-aways" here. The first is that everything must be fulfilled that is written about Jesus in the Law, the Prophets and the Psalms. No further fulfillment of the Law, Prophets and the Psalms was to be forthcoming. It had all occurred. Jesus had already said, concerning John: "The Law and the Prophets were proclaimed until John. Since that time, the good news of the kingdom of God is being preached, and everyone is forcing their way into it." (Luke 16:16) The good news of the kingdom was to be the focus from this point forward.

The second take-away is that the scriptures say that the Messiah will suffer and rise from the dead on the third day. Here was Jesus, the Messiah, as proof that He had risen from the dead on the third day. Jesus then continues to explain that repentance for the forgiveness of sins will be preached in His name to all nations, beginning in Jerusalem. There is a clear tie between the "good news of the kingdom of God" in Luke 16:16 and the repentance for the forgiveness of sins being preached in the name of the Messiah in Luke 24:47.

The third take-away is that the Apostles there assembled are witnesses of "these things." "These things" include the fulfillment of what was written about the Messiah, His suffering, His death and His resurrection from the dead. The Apostles were being commissioned to witness to the world "these things," which collectively are important elements in the "testimony of Jesus." It was left to John to write in Revelation "The testimony of Jesus is the Spirit of Prophecy." (Revelation 19:10)

The fourth take-away is the direct tie between the Father's promise and power from on high. Jesus promised to send "what my Father has promised." He instructed the Apostles to stay in the city (Jerusalem) until you have been clothed with power from on high. The imagery of "clothed with power" makes it clear that

Jesus was describing something external to the Apostles. Clothing is <u>on</u> you, not <u>in</u> you.

When Jesus promised to ask the Father to send the Holy Spirit, he explained:

> *[16] And I will ask the Father, and he will give you another advocate to help you and be with you forever—*
> *[17] the Spirit of truth. The world cannot accept him, because it neither sees him nor knows him. But you know him, for he lives with you and will be in you.*
> John 14:16-17

The Holy Spirit is thus promised by Jesus to be sent from the Father to live in each believer. It is this life that Jesus describes as the abundant life. (John 10:10) Each believer is a temple of God in which the Holy Spirit dwells. (1 Corinthians 3:16) The in-dwelling of the Holy Spirit is what gives eternal life when a believer crosses over from death to life. (See John 5:24)

This indwelling of the Holy Spirit is different from having the Holy Spirit come <u>upon you</u>. Jesus imparted the Holy Spirit to live <u>in</u> the Apostles on Resurrection Sunday. Jesus breathed on his followers and said, "Receive the Holy Spirit." (See John 20:22)

Paul's statement of how to be "saved" contains two "conditions" which need to coincide. (Romans 10:9) A believer must confess with his mouth that Jesus is Lord and believe in his heart that God raised Jesus from the dead. Prior to Resurrection Sunday, each of the disciples had confessed that Jesus was Lord but none had yet believed that God had raised Him from the dead. With the appearance of Jesus in the upper room, they could, for the first time, believe that God had raised Jesus from the dead. With both "conditions" satisfied, Jesus imparted the Holy Spirit to live in them by breathing on them, just as God had breathed the breath of life into Adam at creation. (Genesis 2:7)

Following Resurrection Sunday, Jesus had another discussion with His Apostles.

> *⁴ On one occasion, while he was eating with them, he gave them this command: "Do not leave Jerusalem, but wait for the gift my Father promised, which you have heard me speak about.*
> *⁵ For John baptized with water, but in a few days you will be baptized with the Holy Spirit."*
>
> *⁸ But you will receive power when the Holy Spirit comes on you; and you will be my witnesses in Jerusalem, and in all Judea and Samaria, and to the ends of the earth." (Acts 1:4-5, 8)*

Jesus directly tied the "gift my Father promised" to "baptized with the Holy Spirit." Just as in Luke, there is a promise that the Holy Spirit will come <u>on</u> the Apostles with the result that they will be His witnesses to the ends of the earth. The power they will receive when the Holy Spirit comes upon them is the power necessary to be His witnesses.

Peter at Pentecost

On the day of Pentecost, following the ascension of Jesus into heaven, His disciples were gathered in one place. A sound like a violent wind filled the whole house. They saw tongues of fire that separated and came to rest on each of them. "All of them were filled with the Holy Spirit." (Acts 2:1-4)

When the God-fearing Jews from every nation heard the disciples speaking in the crowd's native languages, Peter was called upon to explain.

> *¹⁵ These people are not drunk, as you suppose. It's only nine in the morning!*
> *¹⁶ No, this is what was spoken by the prophet Joel:*
>
> > *¹⁷ "'In the last days, God says, I will pour out my Spirit on all people. Your sons and daughters will prophesy, your young men will see visions, your old men will dream dreams.*
> > *¹⁸ Even on my servants, both men and women, I will pour out my Spirit in those days, and they will prophesy.*
> > *¹⁹ I will show wonders in the heavens above and signs on the earth below, blood and fire and billows of smoke.*
> > *²⁰ The sun will be turned to darkness and the moon to blood before the coming of the great and glorious day of the Lord.*
> > *²¹ And everyone who calls on the name of the Lord will be saved.'* (Acts 2:15-21)

The prophecy from Joel is the promise of the Father to which Jesus made reference. In that prophecy, God promised to pour out His Spirit <u>on</u> all people, even on His servants. The Father's promise was a general one – "I will pour out my Spirit on all people" – coupled with specific examples of what to expect – "Your sons and daughters will prophesy, your young men will see visions, your old men will dream dreams."

There is no report of any of these examples from Joel that occurred on Pentecost. There is no report that anyone prophesied, that young men saw visions or that old men dreamed dreams. Yet, Peter realized that God had poured out His Spirit on them and they would never be the same. This outpouring of God's Spirit came directly from God and only good things came with it.

There are two other instances in Acts in which God's Spirit was poured out on people who had previously become believers. In Acts 8 the Jerusalem Apostles heard that Samaria had accepted the word of God. According to Jesus' words, this acceptance resulted in eternal life, no condemnation and the passing from death to life described in John 5:24. In spite of the Holy Spirit residing in the new believers in Samaria giving them eternal life, the Jerusalem Apostles dispatched Peter and John to them. Peter and John prayed for them because the Holy Spirit had not yet come upon any of them. (Acts 8:14-17)

In the same fashion, Paul was visiting Ephesus after Apollos had taught there for some time. Paul was led to inquire: "Have you received the Holy Ghost since you believed?" (KJV Acts 19:2) Paul laid his hands on them, the Holy Ghost came on them and they both spoke in tongues and prophesied. The greatest revival of the entire New Testament followed this outpouring of the Holy Spirit on the believers in Ephesus.

A similar outpouring of the Holy Spirit occurred at the House of Cornelius in Chapter 10 of Acts. It is not clear in that report whether Cornelius and his household were already believers prior to Peter's arrival.

What We Know And What We Don't

The Bible accounts concerning Baptism with the Holy Spirit are sparing in detail. There are many theologies which address the specifics of Baptism with the Holy Spirit, what it is, when you can "get it", and how it is obtained and the impact on a believer. For the most part, these theologies arise from the experiences of one or more believers who are attempting to explain their experience.

What we know from the scriptures is that:

- Jesus is the baptizer;
- Power from on high is involved;
- An outpouring of God's Spirit on His people is involved; and
- A profound change should be expected.

Anything more than the foregoing does not appear to be clearly supported by the scriptures. This lack of scriptural support does not, apparently, deter some from teaching a detailed theology of how to receive Baptism with the Holy Spirit, what to expect from Baptism with the Holy Spirit, and whether this phenomenon is still available in the modern age.

I recommend suspicion concerning any theology based upon lack. I am simply not impressed when someone claims that biblical phenomenon no longer occur simply because they have not experienced that phenomenon or only experience it on an occasional basis.

I am much more impressed with theology based upon what Jesus did, rather than what He did not do. If it happened in Jesus life, it should happen today. Otherwise, Jesus is not the same yesterday, today and tomorrow. Jesus said anyone who had faith in Him would do those things He had been doing (not to mention greater things also). (See John 14:12) It does not seem to matter whether this statement is simply a statement of fact or whether it is a command. In either event, somehow the works of Jesus should continue in the lives of believers today.

CHAPTER SIX

What is Baptism With the Holy Spirit?

J esus announced a major paradigm shift that coincided with the appearance of John the Baptist.

> *Truly I tell you, among those born of women there has not risen anyone greater than John the Baptist; yet whoever is least in the kingdom of heaven is greater than he. From the days of John the Baptist until now, the kingdom of heaven has been subjected to violence, and violent people have been raiding it. <u>For all the Prophets and the Law prophesied until John</u>.* (Matthew 11:11-13)

> <u>*The Law and the Prophets were proclaimed until John*</u>. *Since that time, the good news of the kingdom of God is being preached, and everyone is forcing their way into it.* (Luke 16:16)

John's major contribution was to sum up the Law and the Prophets by identifying Jesus as the Messiah, the One who was to come. When Jesus came on the scene the purpose of the Law (to show the need for a savior) and the Prophets (to identify who the Messiah would be) had been accomplished. What remained after Jesus' appearance, death and resurrection was the preaching of the good news of the kingdom of God. The full extent of the Good News will not be revealed until the return of Jesus. However, John announced one aspect of the kingdom that can only be classified as good news.

In all four Gospels, John announced that Jesus would baptize with the Holy Spirit. (Matthew and Luke report John adding that Jesus would baptize with fire.) (Matthew 3:11; Mark 1:7-8; Luke 3:16; and John 1:33-34)

Have you ever wondered why no one said "What on earth are you talking about? Baptize with the Holy Spirit? How does that work? What would that look like? You are a great prophet, explain your statement!"

The scriptures are short on any explanation of what Baptism with the Holy Spirit would look like, how it would work and the practical effect of this baptism.

"Baptism" Not Clear

A search of the Old Testament for the concept of baptism is not very helpful. Since the Old Testament was not written originally in Greek, the word "baptize" is not to be found there. If fact, the English word "baptize" is not a translation of a Greek word but rather a transliteration of the Greek word, *baptizo*. *Baptizo* in the Greek referred to a complete immersion or rendering wholly wet. (And today, we have denominations which argue about the proper methodology for baptism – immersion required or is sprinkling sufficient?)

Although it was not called baptism, ritual washing was observed for multiple reasons in the Jewish community. These various washings included a total immersion in a *mikveh* for some purposes and ritual washing of the hands for other purposes.

The Jews asked Jesus why his disciples did not observe the ritual hand washing before meals. (Matthew 15:1-2) The issue was not a violation of the *law* but rather a *tradition* of the elders. There was no law that required hand washing or total immersion for any purpose. Rather there was a tradition of men for both hand washing and for complete immersion. Men's traditions apparently had nothing to do with the current understanding of baptism as a sacrament in the church.

Jewish full body immersion, when observed, required "living water." For that reason, the full body immersion often took place in a running river or stream. The *mikveh* was one means of providing "living water" for this full body immersion. One instance (among many) for full body immersion was conversion to Judaism. The conversion to Judaism would involve not only a change in "religion" but would amount to transforming someone who was not part of God's Chosen People to a completely different relationship with God.

Becoming one of God's Chosen People would bestow no benefit in an afterlife. Indeed, one of the disputes between the Sadducees and the Pharisees involved whether there was any life after physical death. (The Sadducees did not believe in either a life after death or angels and such beings.)

One of the uses of the *mikveh* was for ritual cleansing following natural bodily functions. In the main, the use of the *mikveh* seems to have had little or no relation to forgiveness of sin.

The requirement for "living water" for ritual immersion may explain why no one found it unusual that John the Baptist was baptizing in the Jordan. Although full body immersion was already used for some purposes, it simply was not called baptism before John.

John baptized with water for repentance. (Matthew 3:11) So far as the scriptures are concerned, this baptism had nothing to do with baptism with the Holy Spirit or with fire. John clarified that he baptized with water but that Jesus would baptize with the Holy Spirit and with fire.

So, what is this baptism with water for repentance? First, let us recognize that the word translated "repentance" comes from the Greek word "*metanoio*" which means to **change your way of thinking**. So, John was saying "I am going to immerse you in water to change your way of thinking." And no one had any questions?

One explanation why there is no question recorded in the Bible about what Baptism with the Holy Spirit might be is that Baptism with the Holy Spirit is a "spiritually discerned" phenomenon that comes from the Spirit of God. As such, it is foolishness to the man without the Spirit. (1 Corinthians 2:14) The man without the Spirit simply cannot understand it.

Many Christians have given Nancy and me a "deer in the headlights" response when we have mentioned Baptism with the Holy Spirit. It is often as if the words simply were not spoken. There is no response. Granted, there is often an unfavorable response from those who have been exposed to some of the abuses taught in the name of Baptism with the Holy Spirit. However, more often there simply is no response at all.

It is well recognized that people often do not comprehend what they just heard. Their hearing was not impaired but understanding was completely lacking.

I recall vividly a teaching I heard in person from Bill Johnson, senior pastor of Bethel Church in Redding, California, about creating and maintaining a culture for miracles. Nancy and I both were simply blown away with the significance and truth of what we had just heard. Some weeks later we listened once again to a CD presentation from the very same Bill Johnson on the very same issue. He explained the idea in nearly identical terms as we had just heard. We were amazed to find that we had first heard this message nearly one entire year before we heard it again in person. The message made no impact on either of us the first time through and yet made a profound impact one year later.

One of the ministries of the Holy Spirit is to quicken our hearts and minds to receive the truth of a message when He has prepared us to hear and comprehend it. This quickening of our minds is why the scriptures are accurately described as the living word. What can be entirely meaningless when heard the first time can, upon a later reading or exposure, constitute the most profound truth we have heard in our lives.

It is this same quickening that caused each of our group of Episcopal friends to react with such amazement to realize we had been confessing our individual belief in the Holy Spirit as the *Lord and Giver of Life* in the Nicene Creed. In my case, I had said so every Sunday during the Episcopal liturgy for many, many years. Until I experienced the Holy Spirit as Lord and Giver of Life, I simply had never comprehended that the language even existed in the Nicene Creed.

We may be seeing the same phenomenon in the new disciples at Ephesus described in Acts 19. When Paul visited them they had been instructed by Appollos and had become believers. Paul, perhaps understanding the inability to comprehend spiritually discerned things without the Spirit, asked a profound question, "Have you received the Holy Ghost since you believed?" (Acts 19:2 KJV)

The new disciples' response perhaps reflected a shortcoming of Apollos' teaching and perhaps reflected their inability to comprehend spiritually discerned matters that come from the Spirit of God. They responded, "No, we have not even heard that there is a Holy Spirit." Irrespective of the source of the problem, Paul's solution was to introduce them to a baptism different from John's baptism.

When Paul had baptized them in the name of the Lord Jesus, he then laid hands on them at which point the Holy Spirit came on them, and they spoke in tongues and prophesied. (Acts 19:6)

What followed in the Church at Ephesus was, perhaps the greatest revival recorded in the Bible. In about two years time, the conviction was so great that all the Jews and Greeks who lived in province of Asia heard the word of the Lord. During this time, God did extraordinary miracles through Paul. (Just exactly which miracles are not extraordinary?)

Many who practiced sorcery publicly burned their scrolls. The value of the scrolls is recorded at fifty thousand drachma. A drachma was equivalent to one day's wage. Thus, fifty thousand drachma would equal one man's wages for 136.9863 years. That is just five days short of 137 years. Now that is a revival!

Wrong Expectations

The Jews expected the Messiah to be a conquering hero who would restore the nation of Israel to its former status. The Jews longed for and expected to be freed from Roman occupation. They awaited the Messiah to bring this great liberation and victory to pass. What would be more natural than to associate Baptism with the Holy spirit and with fire with overthrowing the Roman occupation?

The Hebrew word *messiah* and the Greek word *christos* both mean the anointed one. The expectation was that God's anointing on a man would carry with it supernatural strength, wisdom and power to effect a magnificent change for God's Chosen People.

The Apostles (and likely even John the Baptist) misapprehended the nature of the kingdom that Jesus brought with Him. Just before Jesus ascended to heaven, he explained to the Apostles, "*I am going to send you what my Father has promised; but stay in the city until you have been clothed with power from on high.*" (Luke 24:49) This promise of power certainly would evoke the desire for the oppression of Rome to be overcome.

> *Then they gathered around him and asked him, "Lord, are you at this time going to restore the kingdom to Israel?"* Acts 1:4-6

The Father's promise was power from on high. Rather than understand that Jesus was going to make available to them the power of the Holy Spirit (power from on high) upon which He had relied during all of his public ministry with them, the Apostles jumped immediately to the Jewish default understanding of the function of the Messiah, restoration of the kingdom to Israel.

What Jesus promised to send was "what my Father has promised." The promise of the Father referred to here is the outpouring of His Spirit on all people. (Joel 2:28-29) The last part of the Father's promise is that "everyone who calls on the name of the Lord will be saved. (Joel 2:32) These verses from Joel, coupled with the promise in Luke, show that power from on high was to be made available when God pours out His Spirit on all people.

Apparently it took the actual Baptism with the Holy Spirit recorded in Acts 2 for the Apostles to comprehend what Jesus was addressing. So long as they were men without the Spirit, they were unable to comprehend spiritual things.

Was John the Baptist Confused Also?

Even John the Baptist didn't understand what the Messiah was going to do.[3] Scripture records clearly that John recognized Jesus as the Messiah yet at one point he sent two of his disciples to ask Jesus if He was the one to come or should Israel expect another. Let's take a closer look at this question.

In Chapter 7 of Luke we read the account of the centurion in Capernaum whose servant was sick and about to die. Jesus at first set out to visit the ailing servant. While on the way, a discussion ensued with the centurion who demonstrated his great faith in the authority Jesus carried. The result was the healing of the servant without the personal intervention of Jesus.

This account is followed by Jesus' actions at a funeral procession outside the village of Nain. Jesus was being followed not only by His disciples but also by a large crowd of others. The healing of the centurion's servant had expanded the crowd who went from place to place with Jesus.

In addition, there was a large crowd of townspeople of Nain who were part of the funeral procession for the widow of Nain's son. Jesus approached the funeral bier. He told the young man, who happened to be dead, to get up. Luke records that "the dead man sat up and began to talk, and Jesus gave him back to his mother." (Luke 7:15)

The combined crowds were filled with awe – and why not? They praised God – no suggestion here that Jesus was calling upon Beelzebub. "A great prophet has appeared among us,' they said. 'God has come to help his people.'" (Luke 7:16) Surely the

---

[3] I heard this suggestion in a talk by Steve Thompson in a message recorded on CD and distributed by Morning Star Ministries. I am indebted to him for the idea.

report was carried on all the major channels, as well as CNN, MSNBC and Fox News, with film at eleven. Don't you know there was some serious shouting when the young man sat up?

John's disciples reported to John in prison how Jesus had healed the centurion's servant and raised from the dead the widow of Nain's son. John was the one appointed and anointed by God Himself to recognize and identify Jesus as the Messiah. Yet, he apparently had questions.

John's response is extraordinary. Calling two of his disciples, John sent them to Jesus to ask, *"Are you the one who is to come, or should we expect someone else?"* (Luke 7:20)

Apparently John the Baptist expected extraordinary (and perhaps theretofore unseen) power to accompany Baptism with the Holy Spirit. John knew about God's healing power. (Namaan's healing from leprosy in 2 Kings 5:1-13). He likewise knew of the instance when Elisha raised the Shunammite's Son to life. (2 Kings 4:32-36) The things reported about Jesus had occurred previously in Israel's history.

John had no question that Jesus was to Baptize with the Holy Spirit. He expected demonstrations of power unlike any experienced in the history of Israel to accompany this power. The one who would Baptize with the Holy Spirit would surely be able to do more than these reports illustrated.

Just as John the Baptist may have been confused about what to expect from Baptism with the Holy Spirit, many today are confused and a little frightened when they consider what may happen to one who is Baptized with the Holy Spirit.

Since Baptism with the Holy Spirit is uniformly described as a "baptism" by both John and Jesus, we should expect some similarities to baptism with water. The Greek word *baptizo* refers to immersion of the thing baptized. If you are baptized in water, you become thoroughly wet. However, becoming thoroughly wet is not the goal of baptism with water. The goal is the spiritual change that accompanies the decision to become baptized coupled with the obedience to participate in baptism.

Baptism with the Holy Spirit is not spiritual Brylcreme ("a little dab will do ya"). God gives His Holy Spirit without limit. (John 3:34) The Father gives His Holy Spirit to all those who ask Him. (Luke 11: 10- 13)Baptism with the Holy Spirit, then, should result in one becoming thoroughly immersed in the Holy Spirit. When God pours out His Spirit on His people, they don't get only a little dab.

The Greek word *baptizo* is often used when referring to dyeing cloth. The cloth is *baptizo'd* (to make up a word) in the dye. The result is a change in the essential makeup of the cloth. The cloth does not retain its original color on the inside with only the outside being affected. Rather, a white sweater dyed red will be red inside and out. Cut the strands of the knitting and you will find that each thread is now red.

Just as baptism with water has a more important spiritual effect in addition to the physical attribute of becoming thoroughly wet, Baptism with the Holy Spirit has a spiritual effect that has little to do with any physical aspects. When Jesus was Baptized with the Holy Spirit, John saw the Holy Spirit descend as a dove upon Him <u>and remain</u>. (John 1:33) God's intention is that His presence will be available to us at all times. That is, He will abide with us.

Our goal following Baptism with the Holy Spirit should be to host the Presence of God. Often, believer's ask one another whether each has been Baptized with the Holy Spirit. This is exactly what Paul asked the twelve new disciples in Ephesus when he visited while Apollos was at Corinth. "Have you received the Holy Ghost since you believed?" (Acts 19:2 KJV) For a new believer, this may be a relevant question. For more "mature" believers, the question smacks too much of history and not enough of continuity.

When you meet someone for the first time, you may inquire whether he/she is married. In essence you are asking whether there was a wedding in their past. The more important question is not the historical wedding but rather the status of the relationship today. Is the spouse still living? What is the health and vibrancy of the relationship?

So it is with Baptism with the Holy Spirit. The important question is the status of the relationship. When the Holy Spirit came <u>upon you</u>, did you invite Him to remain? Do you have daily conversation with Him? Whose agenda are the two of you following? Who has the laboring oar in your collective boat?

Baptism with the Holy Spirit is not a destination. When God pours out His Spirit upon you, you have not "arrived." Don't expect to spend the remainder of your days in that place. You have places to go and people to see if you are going to follow the Holy Spirit's agenda for your life.

Baptism with the Holy Spirit is more like a launching pad. The launching pad is where the rocket abides, but it abides there for the sole purpose of going somewhere else on its next mission.

Only by "putting on" the rocket can you experience its power. You will never get to the moon by standing next to Apollo 11. No matter how many space travels you participate in, no matter how many times you walk on the moon, you will not be able to fly without the rocket. The power always resides in the rocket, not in the astronaut. By ourselves, we can do nothing. The branch does not bear any fruit unless it remains in the vine. (John 15:4-5)

Although men seem to "worship" the astronauts, the truth is they are nothing without the rocket. True, they have learned to reside in the rocket and rely upon its power. True, they have learned how to co-labor with the rocket by providing some guidance. However, those super-star astronauts are just earth-bound guys without the rocket. In a very real sense, they have just been carried along for the ride.

CHAPTER SEVEN

Baptism with the Holy Spirit and "Spiritual Gifts"

The relationship between Baptism with the Holy Spirit and "Gifts of the Holy Spirit" is the subject of considerable debate. The connotation of the English word "gifts" can easily be confusing when the intent is to describe the result of Baptism with the Holy Spirit. Referring to certain spiritual matters as "gifts" is extra-biblical and should, therefore, be used with care.

In most instances, referring to spiritual matters as "gifts" is harmless and corresponds to mainline language usage. However, there are potentially confusing aspects to use of the word "gifts."

In contemporary English the word "gift" or "gifts" often refers to something transferred without cost from one person to another with no strings attached. Thus, it is proper to say, "If you have to work for it, it is not a gift."

The giver relinquishes complete control of "Gifts" and the receiver thereafter has total ownership. This type of gift may be used at the receiver's sole discretion. While appropriate to describe birthday presents, it is not at all accurate for describing what biblical scholars refer to as "gifts of the Holy Spirit."

"Gifts" may also describe a physical or mental *ability*. This is entirely appropriate English usage when describing, for example, a photographic memory or superior eye-hand coordination. That type of memory is a gift in the sense that it is not received in payment of wages but rather is part of someone's toolkit due to a divine deposit. In this context, the "gift" can often be improved by repetition, training, and experience. However, the initial presence or absence of the gift is completely beyond the person's control. The owner of the ability may use it or not at his whim. It is not at all accurate to apply this understanding of "gifts" to the concept biblical scholars refer to as "gifts of the Holy Spirit."

Baptism with the Holy Spirit is most often linked to a "laundry list" of "spiritual gifts." (1 Corinthians 12) There is no direct scriptural connection between Baptism with the Holy Spirit and this "laundry list." I am not saying there is no connection between Baptism with the Holy Spirit and the laundry list. Rather, I am saying there is no direct scriptural link.

The matters on the "laundry list" are not described as "gifts" in the original Greek. Rather, the "laundry list" contains matters each described as a "manifestation of the Spirit." The Spirit distributes these manifestations just as He determines. (1 Corinthians 12:11)

Accuracy in the use of the language of the scripture helps us understand the nature of the "laundry list." The description of the items as manifestations of the Holy Spirit helps avoid an inappropriate (and therefore confusing) understanding of "gifts" as either a present (completely relinquished by the giver and subject to the control of the receiver) or a physical/mental ability (imparted from birth as part of the overall package that is you).

Scripture describes various ways in which the Holy Spirit manifests Himself in the ordinary circumstances of our lives. Scripture does not describe items or abilities that somehow become intrinsic to the believer.

So What Does Scripture Really Say?

When our minds were renewed, we began to look critically at the Word to determine what it really said. I was no longer content to rely upon the sermons I had heard, the books I had read and anecdotal information from other Christians. I wanted to know what Jesus said about any issue.

It has not been uncommon for me to discover that the language of the Bible did not support what I had been taught and what I had heard. When we started teaching and presenting information on miracles, signs and wonders, it became immediately obvious that there was a plethora of teachings and understandings about the "gifts of the Spirit."

Since Nancy and I had an explosion in our experience of the percentage and number of people who were healed on the spot while we (and others) prayed for them, our friends, pastors and leaders assigned various labels to us.

It was common to have a pastor (or other mature Christian) single us out as having the gift of healing. The either stated or implied connotation in most instances was that we had received power from on high to operate in a healing ministry. We became the "go to" folks in certain circles for healing. This trend made us very uncomfortable.

It was nice to receive some notice that miraculous encounters seemed to follow us. However, neither Nancy nor I felt that we had a special gift that was any different from what could be experienced by all believers.

I was so aware that it wasn't me that was doing anything, I was fairly certain that it must be Nancy (or one or more of the friends we invited to pray with us). I was not sure which of them had the "gift" but I knew it wasn't me.

Much to my surprise, Nancy (and our other friends) had the same certainty that it wasn't her. Who, then, was it who had this "gift" of healing?

The distribution of the manifestations is the sole province of the Holy Spirit. (1 Corinthians 12:11) No matter what the manifestation, it is the work of "one and the same Spirit."

It is comforting to know that the Holy Spirit performs His work through manifestations of the Holy Spirit. He is never looking for a manifestation of Jeffie.

The only ability the Holy Spirit seeks in believers is "avail" (yes, put down the dictionary, I made it up). Availability is all He requires. He will supply the rest – better than we can ask or imagine.

Language Difficulties from 1 Corinthians 12

The King James Version of 1 Corinthians 12:1 says: "Now concerning spiritual *gifts*, brethren, I would not have you ignorant." The word "gifts" is rendered in italics indicating the word has been added by the translators. That is, the Greek words of that sentence do not include one which can be translated "gifts." The translators rendered *pneumatikos*, an adjective, as "spiritual *gifts.*" The adjective means spiritual but there is no noun in the Greek for it to modify. The addition of the word "gifts" is unfortunate because the first three verses of this twelfth chapter have nothing to do with "gifts."

The NIV translation of 1 Corinthians 12:1 adds even more emphasis to "gifts": "*Now about the gifts of the Spirit, brothers and sisters, I do not want you to be uninformed.*" A more literal translation is: "Now about spiritual matters, brothers and sisters, I do not want you to be uninformed." I recognize there is no noun to be translated "matters," just like there is no noun to be translated "gifts." The verses which follow fit much more closely with "matters" than with "gifts."

In the following verse 3, Paul talks about diversities of three categories: gifts, administrations and operations. The emphasis in those three verses is that there is but one Spirit, Lord and God. Verse six completes the contrast between the one True God and idols worshiped by the Gentiles.

When "gifts" is used in verse 4, the Greek word is *charisma*, which refers to a special spiritual endowment, religious qualification or miraculous faculty. This is the Greek word from which the term "charismatic" is derived.

Interestingly enough, "charismatic" is commonly used to describe someone who has natural characteristics, abilities and a vivacious personality. A "charismatic" person is someone to whom others will look for leadership and guidance.

The spiritual revival of the 1960's gave birth to the tag "charismatic church," referring to congregations who were influenced by a relationship with the Holy Spirit. The charismatic church has placed much emphasis on "flowing in the gifts," "walking in the gifts," and "operating in the gifts" of the Holy Spirit. It is now common place to refer to the laundry list of 1 Corinthians 12:7-10 as "charismatic gifts" or "gifts of the Holy Spirit."

The fourteenth chapter of 1 Corinthians further compounds this emphasis on "gifts." "Follow the way of love and eagerly desire gifts of the Spirit, especially prophecy." (1 Corinthians 14:1) As before, no Greek word for "gifts' can be found here. Just as in 1 Corinthians 12:1, *pneumatikos* is used as an adjective in this verse and there is no noun to be modified.

Verse 12 of Chapter 14 sheds more light on this subject. "*So it is with you. Since you are eager for gifts of the Spirit, try to excel in those that build up the church.*" As the King James version puts it: "*Even so ye, forasmuch as ye are zealous of spiritual gifts seek that ye may excel to the edifying of the church.*" (1 Corinthians 14:12)

In this fourteenth chapter, the Greek word translated "spiritual" in the King James Version (then with "gifts" added) is *pneuma*, not *pneumatikos*. *Pneuma* is a noun while *pneumatikos* is an adjective. An adjective begs for a noun to modify. Thus, there is desire to complete the idea of spiritual something (unspecified). However, a noun does not modify another noun. Thus, *pneuma* should not be transformed from a noun meaning Spirit to an adjective that is incomplete. A translation of 1 Corinthians 14:12 that would reflect the noun/adjective problem identified above would be: "Since you are eager for the Spirit, seek that you may excel in building up the church." Building up the Body of Christ (the Church) is a primary focus of the Holy Spirit.

What About the Laundry List

Let's look at how the NIV translators present the "laundry list." Note, the laundry list items are not described as gifts but rather as manifestations of the Spirit.

> [7] Now to each one the <u>manifestation of the Spirit</u> is given <u>for the common good</u>.
> [8] To one there is given through the Spirit a message of wisdom, to another a message of knowledge by means of the same Spirit,

*⁹ to another faith by the same Spirit, to another gifts
of healing ⁴ by that one Spirit,
¹⁰ to another miraculous powers, to another prophecy,
to another distinguishing between spirits, to another
speaking in different kinds of tongues, and to still
another the interpretation of tongues.
¹¹ <u>All these are the work of one and the same Spirit,</u>
and <u>he distributes them</u> to each one, <u>just as he
determines</u>.* 1 Corinthians 12:7-11

What is a manifestation of the Spirit? The Greek word
translated "manifestation" is *phanerosis*, meaning an exhibition
or expression. Thus, a message (word) of knowledge received as
a manifestation of the Holy Spirit is an appearance (exhibition)
or expression of the Holy Spirit. The Holy Spirit gives "legs"
to the "word" by entrusting it to one or more believers for the
accomplishment of His purposes in the circumstances.

The Holy Spirit distributes this manifestation to members
of the Body of Christ according to His determination. The
distribution is necessary to accomplish His purposes, which are
always for the common good. He chooses who will "hear and
report" the word of knowledge in that particular group.

The recipient(s) of the word of knowledge is the person(s)
chosen by the Holy Spirit at the time from that group. Change
the group and you may well see a different person receiving the
word of knowledge.

The Holy Spirit will not permit his purposes to be frustrated
by the absence from the group of any particular "gifted" person
who has heard a message from Him on a prior occasion. In other
words, receiving a word of knowledge on one occasion is not an

---

⁴ Actually, both words are plural, that is, <u>gifts of healings</u>.

indication that the receiver will always receive a future word of knowledge.

It is not uncommon to have several believers in a group "hear" the same word of knowledge in any particular circumstance. Thus, if one hearer "sits on it", the message still can be delivered by the others who heard.

The Holy Spirit does not manifest His presence by a word of knowledge solely to amuse or entertain us. Rather, He has a purpose for the manifestation.

Any particular manifestations will work together as can be seen from the following example.

- Believer A receives a word of knowledge; thus, he knows something now he has not learned but that has been revealed to him.
- Believer B receives a word of wisdom; thus he knows by revelation the best application of action for that word of knowledge; and
- Believer C receives faith; thus he has, in this instance, the faith to say, "We can do that and I will start."
- Believer D receives a distinguishing between spirits; thus he recognizes the presence of a demonic presence in the circumstance and uses his authority as a believer to demand the unclean spirit to leave.

No Power Personal to the Receiver

As pointed out in Chapter Two, the actor with the laboring oar in all spiritual matters is the Holy Spirit, God Himself, not me. Any suggestion that Baptism with the Holy Spirit imparts any power **personal to the receiver** and **available upon demand** should be quickly rejected. The trolley car must stay on the tracks or risk being separated from the source of power. Further, the power resides in the source and simply manifests itself in movement of the trolley along pre-determined paths.

Other Confusing Aspects of "Gifts"

The laundry list of <u>manifestations</u> of the Holy Spirit is not the same reference as the use of the word "gifts" in 1 Corinthians 12:4, which says: *"Now there are diversities of gifts but the same Spirit."* (KJV) The word translated there as "gifts" is *charisma*, an altogether different concept from *phanerosis*.

The *charisma* referenced in 1 Corinthians 12:4 are further explained by Paul in Romans 12:6-13 (KJV):

> [6] *Having then gifts differing according to the grace that is given to us, whether prophecy, let us prophesy according to the proportion of faith;*
> [7] *Or ministry, let us wait on our ministering: or he that teacheth, on teaching;*
> [8] *Or he that exhorteth, on exhortation: he that giveth, let him do it with simplicity; he that ruleth, with diligence; he that sheweth mercy, with cheerfulness.*
> [9] *Let love be without dissimulation. Abhor that which is evil; cleave to that which is good.*
> [10] *Be kindly affectioned one to another with brotherly love; in honour preferring one another;*
> [11] *Not slothful in business; fervent in spirit; serving the Lord;*
> [12] *Rejoicing in hope; patient in tribulation; continuing instant in prayer;*
> [13] *Distributing to the necessity of saints; given to hospitality.*

These "gifts," then, include prophecy, ministry, teaching, exhortation, giving, ruling, mercy, love, abhorrence of the bad, love of the good, brotherly love, honoring others, avoiding sloth, fervency in spirit, serving the Lord, rejoicing in hope, patience, distributing to the necessity of saints and hospitality. This is not an exhaustive list but rather simple examples of unearned grace poured out on believers and distributed as the Holy Spirit deems fit.

Avoid Needless Confusion

There is no universal agreement about the identity of the Gifts of the Holy Spirit. The Catechism of the Catholic Church lists seven gifts of the Holy Spirit, including wisdom, understanding, counsel, knowledge, fortitude, piety, and fear of the Lord (wonder and awe). (See Isaiah 11:1-2)

These seven gifts of the Holy Spirit are likewise listed in the Book of Common Prayer (1927) for the Episcopal liturgy for Confirmation. That particular liturgy began with the report in Acts 8 of Peter and John going to the new believers at Samaria who had received the word of God. Peter and John prayed "that they might receive the Holy Ghost: for as yet he was fallen upon none of them: only they were baptized in the name of the Lord Jesus." (Acts 8:15-16 KJV)

These Samaritan believers had been baptized when they believed Philip who was preaching things concerning the kingdom of God and the name of Jesus Christ. (Acts 8:12) In spite of this baptism, the Apostles in Jerusalem believed another step was available (and perhaps even necessary). Thus, Peter and John were dispatched.

Peter and John laid their hands on them and they received the Holy Ghost. (Acts 8:17) Most current thinking on this occurrence is that it is a report of Baptism with the Holy Spirit. The 1927

Episcopal understanding of what was imparted through this baptism was the listing of the seven fold spirits of God of Isaiah 11:1-2, not the laundry list of 1 Corinthians 12 or the listing of gifts in Romans 12.

The Episcopal liturgy for Confirmation from 1927 includes this prayer:

> "Strengthen them, we beseech thee O Lord, with the Holy Ghost, the Comforter, and daily increase in them thy manifold gifts of grace: the spirit of wisdom and understanding, the spirit of counsel and ghostly strength, the spirit of knowledge and true godliness; and fill them, O Lord, with the spirit of thy holy fear, now and for ever. Amen."

Inappropriate Use of the Word "Gifts"

It is not uncommon to hear Christians claim to have received certain "gifts" but not others. It is likewise not uncommon to hear pastors single out members of their congregation who "have" or "operate in" certain named "gifts." Some believers seem to believe that they have been given a "personal power gift." That is, they believe that one with the "gift of healing" has power peculiar to him/her that can be exercised at the will of the person. Let us quickly dispel that myth. The power always resides with the Holy Spirit. The work is always done by the Holy Spirit. Any claim to the contrary is simply incorrect.

There is a specific danger associated with this misconception. Nancy and I have often been singled out in a congregation as "having" or "operating in" or "walking in" the gift of healing. While it is true that the Holy Spirit often manifests the healing that Jesus bought and paid for in the body of the person for

69

whom we pray, we have no power to accomplish anything of the sort. We heal no one. Yet, this "identification" of us as having this particular "gift" seems to create an atmosphere among the congregation that can perhaps be described as "We have our 'gifted' people here today so those who are sick in their bodies should seek them out for prayer." The rest of the congregation seems to feel, at that time, that they are excused from co-laboring with God in the area of healing of body, soul and spirit because the "pros" are here.

The Holy Spirit manifests through all believers, not only a select few. The Lord is always asking, "Whom shall I send? And who will go for us?" (Isaiah 6:8) He awaits an Isaiah response, "Here I am. Send Me." (Isaiah 6:9)

We find ourselves, as believers, in the same position Isaiah occupied before he was sent. Our guilt has been taken away and our sin is atoned for. (Isaiah 6:7) Therefore, just as Isaiah was "deemed worthy" to carry the message of God, so are all believers.

Charismatic churches and denominations point to 1 Corinthians 12:7-10 for the laundry list discussed previously in this chapter, which they identify as Gifts of the Spirit.

Those who emphasize the "five-fold" ministry often refer to apostles, prophets, teachers, miracles, gifts of healing, helps, guidance and tongues as "gifts of the Spirit." (See 1 Corinthians 12:28)

To further confuse the issue, Paul lists the fruits of the Spirit as love, joy, peace, longsuffering, gentleness, goodness, faith, meekness, and self-control. (Galatians 5:22-23)

Much theology has developed to distinguish between the groupings of "gifts" and differentiation between "gifts" and "fruit." For each theological suggestion, there are usually multiple "scholars" who disagree.

Not only is there disagreement about the identity and nature of the "gifts/fruit" but there is widespread disagreement how the individual believer receives this grace, and at what stage of his/her spiritual walk.

It is widely accepted that the Holy Spirit lives **in** born again believers. It is likewise widely accepted that you receive the "whole" Holy Spirit, not a partial Holy Spirit (because the Holy Spirit is a person, not an idea or an influence).

There is a significant difference of opinion whether there is a "second experience" following salvation at which time the Holy Spirit comes **upon** the believer.

Bill Johnson, senior pastor of Bethel Church in Redding, California, teaches that the Holy Spirit is **in** all believers but is not **on** all believers. He explains that the Holy Spirit is **in** you for your benefit but **on** you for the benefit of others.

The Bible is simply short on explanation of how Baptism with the Holy Spirit looks in everyday clothes.

CHAPTER EIGHT

How Do I Get Baptized with the Holy Spirit?

The Bible does not contain a formula for Baptism with the Holy Spirit. There are no words "in red" that we can repeat. Even the examples we see are not consistent.

It seems clear that Baptism with the Holy Spirit is properly described as the promise of the Father. Jesus admonished the Apostles to wait for "the promise of the Father" (KJV) or "the gift my Father promised" (NIV) and described that promise by saying "you will be baptized with the Holy Spirit." (Acts 1:4-5)

Jesus offered a further explanation. "You will receive power when the Holy Spirit comes on you; and you will be my witnesses in Jerusalem, and in all Judea and Samaria, and to the ends of the earth." (Acts 1:7)

The First Instance

Peter explained what happened when the Holy Spirit came upon them at Pentecost. "This is what was spoken by the prophet Joel." (Acts 2:16)

> *17 "'In the last days, God says, I will pour out my Spirit on all people. Your sons and daughters will prophesy, your young men will see visions, your old men will dream dreams.*
> *18 Even on my servants, both men and women, I will pour out my Spirit in those days, and they will prophesy.*
> *19 I will show wonders in the heavens above and signs on the earth below, blood and fire and billows of smoke.*
> *20 The sun will be turned to darkness and the moon to blood before the coming of the great and glorious day of the Lord.*
> *21 And everyone who calls on the name of the Lord will be saved.'* (Acts 2:17-21)

The Bible does not report that the disciples saw visions, dreamed dreams or prophesied. There is no report of wonders in the heavens and signs on the earth below, blood and fire and billows of smoke. The sun was not turned to darkness nor the moon turned to blood. However, the Bible is clear that there was suddenly a sound of violent wind coming from heaven that filled the whole house. They saw tongues of fire that separated and came to rest on each of them. "All of them were filled with the Holy Spirit and began to speak in other tongues as the Spirit enabled them." (Acts 2:4)

Wind and fire have particular significance. God's messengers (angels) are described as winds. God's servants (angels) are described as flames of fire. (Psalm 104:4) Peter recognized the significance of these supernatural phenomena as God pouring out His Spirit on all men as prophesied by Joel. Even though the manifestations were different, the essence was evident to Peter.

Significantly (or not), no one is reported to have laid hands on any of those who were baptized with the Holy Spirit on this day. Nor is it reported that any of the disciples had specifically requested Baptism with the Holy Spirit. Recall, however, that they were all in one place, praying, waiting as Jesus had instructed.

Peter and John and the Samarians

When Philip had baptized some Samarians there was no recognized outpouring of God's Spirit on them. The Samarian crowds had seen signs performed by Philip. Impure spirits were driven out of many, the paralyzed or lame were being healed and great joy was found in the city. Upon hearing that Samarians had accepted the word of god, Peter and John were dispatched. Peter and John first prayed for the new believers and then "placed their hands on them." (Acts 8:17) The Samarians received the Holy Spirit, an occasion which was very impressive to Simon the sorcerer who then offered money for the ability to impart the Holy Spirit by the laying on of hands.

This report does not look like either the prophesy of Joel or the first instance on Pentecost. Yet, there was such an awareness of God's Spirit being poured out that Simon wanted to buy the ability. Although it looked and sounded different, there can be little question "this is that which was promised by the Father." The Spirit was poured out on believers who had already been baptized.

House of Cornelius

Cornelius was a centurion in the Italian Regiment. Although he and all his family were devout and God-fearing, they had not been baptized in water. Cornelius had a vision in which he distinctly saw an angel who informed him that his prayers and gifts to the poor had come up as a memorial offering before God and he should send for Simon Peter who was that day in Joppa.

Although Jewish tradition prohibited a Jew from entering a gentile's home, Peter came when bidden and spoke with the assembled household. He told them the best one sentence synopsis of the entire New Testament. He said, *"You know what has happened throughout the province of Judea, beginning in Galilee after the baptism that John preached – how God anointed Jesus of Nazareth with the Holy Spirit and power, and how he went around doing good and healing all who were under the power of the devil, because God was with him."* (Act 10:38)

While Peter continued speaking, "the Holy Spirit came on all who heard the message." (Acts 10:44) The Jews with Peter were astonished to see that the Holy Spirit had been poured out on Gentiles who they heard speaking in tongues and praising God.

Peter's response was to baptize Cornelius and his household in water because they had already received the Holy Spirit "just as we have." (Acts 10:47-48) Following the baptism, Peter again violated Jewish tradition by staying with Cornelius and his household for a few days.

This time there is no report of wind, fire, signs in the heavens, prophesying, dreams or visions. Yet, all knew that "this was that." Not only "this was that" but there was no requirement that Peter or anyone in his entourage lay hands on Cornelius' household. In spite of this "liturgical irregularity," Cornelius and his household were Baptized with the Holy Spirit. It is interesting to note that Cornelius received his angelic visitation prior to either his Holy Spirit or water baptism.

Ephesus

Apollos enjoyed some success in Ephesus. Twelve believers were baptized in water in response to his teaching.

When Apollos was visiting Corinth, Paul visited Ephesus. When he encountered the new believers he inquired, *"Have you received the Holy Ghost since you believed?"* (Acts 19:2 KJV)

Paul explained that John baptized with the baptism of repentance, imploring the people to believe on Jesus. The Ephesian believers were then baptized in the name of the Lord Jesus. "And when Paul laid his hands upon them, the Holy Ghost came on them; and they spake with tongues, and prophesied." (Acts 19:5-6 KJV)

Following this experience, Paul remained for two years during which the greatest revival recorded in the Bible occurred.

Clearly, "this was that" except that it was different, again. No wind, no fire, some prophesying, no signs in the heavens and Paul did lay his hands on them.

Conclusions

The best conclusion is that there is no "scriptural formula" for Baptism with the Holy Spirit. However, some guidelines can be discerned from other portions of the scripture.

Lay on Hands?

Laying on hands is a traditional method of imparting blessings from God. We see it in Acts 8 and Acts 19. We may not have seen it in Acts 10 at Cornelius' house simply because Cornelius and his household didn't wait until the end of the sermon. They "jumped the gun." We may not have seen it in Acts 2 simply because there was no one present who had any idea what was about to happen. All were "tarrying" in Jerusalem.

Jesus is the Baptizer. Our hands are not required. Since we are part of the cloud of witness, it seems our hands should be a recommendation.

We can be certain that laying on hands is not a disqualifier since both Peter and John in Samaria and Paul in Ephesus found this to be an efficacious method of imparting this blessing.

Someone Should Ask

By definition, a paraclete is one summoned along side. If you want the Paraclete, you should summon Him.

In none of the examples from Acts do we have a report of an overt request by the person(s) being baptized. It seems to stretch credulity to contend that the persons being Baptized with the Holy Spirit were not asking to be immersed with the Holy Spirit. Just by his presence in the situation it can safely be asserted that each was asking to be baptized. No one attending a basketball game specifically asks for the jump ball to begin the game but all have come for that purpose.

Jesus had a lot to say about asking.

He Doesn't Say No.

> *7 "Ask and it will be given to you; seek and you will find; knock and the door will be opened to you.*
> *8 For everyone who asks receives; the one who seeks finds; and to the one who knocks, the door will be opened.*
> *9 "Which of you, if your son asks for bread, will give him a stone?*

*¹⁰ Or if he asks for a fish, will give him a snake?
¹¹ If you, then, though you are evil, know how to give good gifts to your children, how much more will your Father in heaven give good gifts to those who ask him!* (Matthew 7:7-11)

The tense and verb form of the action verbs here – ask, seek and knock – can best be translated as "ask and keep on asking" etc. The promise is universal. <u>Everyone</u> who asks receives. Surely God's Holy Spirit being poured out on His people qualifies as a "good gift" from God. Finally, we know that Baptism with the Holy Spirit is good because God only gives good gifts.

The promise is not for generic "good gifts" only but specifically includes the Holy Spirit. *If you then, though you are evil, know how to give good gifts to your children, how much more will your Father in heaven give the Holy Spirit to those who ask him!*" (Luke 11:13)

<u>Agreement Seals the Deal</u>.

There is power in agreement in the kingdom. If you and I agree about your asking for Baptism with the Holy Spirit, He has promised to deliver.

*¹⁹ "Again, truly I tell you that if two of you on earth agree about anything they ask for, it will be done for them by my Father in heaven.
²⁰ For where two or three gather in my name, there am I with them."* (Matthew 18:19-20)

Ask Believing You Will Receive.

There should be no question in your mind that God will pour out his Spirit on those who ask. Don't look for specific confirmation but rather trust that "this is that."

> *²⁴ Therefore I tell you, whatever you ask for in prayer, believe that you have received it, and it will be yours.* (Mark 11:24)

Power Depends Upon Unity with Jesus.

Jesus placed a premium on unity with Him. His unity with the Father meant that He was in the Father and the Father was in Him. Thus, there was no conflict. This unity promoted Jesus' ability to discern (see) what the Father was doing so that He could do that.

Jesus desires the same unity with us. We are to abide (remain) in Him as the branch abides in the vine.

> *¹ I am the true vine, and my Father is the husbandman.*
> *² Every branch in me that beareth not fruit he taketh away: and every branch that beareth fruit, he purgeth it, that it may bring forth more fruit.*
> *³ Now ye are clean through the word which I have spoken unto you.*
> *⁴ Abide in me, and I in you. As the branch cannot bear fruit of itself, except it abide in the vine; no more can ye, except ye abide in me.*
> *⁵ I am the vine, ye are the branches: He that abideth in me, and I in him, the same bringeth forth much fruit: for without me ye can do nothing.*

⁷ If ye abide in me, and my words abide in you, ye shall ask what ye will, and it shall be done unto you. ⁸ Herein is my Father glorified, that ye bear much fruit; so shall ye be my disciples. John 15:1-8 (KJV)

The nature of the relationship of the branch to the vine is instructive. The life giving power and the power to produce fruit resides in the vine, not the branch. Separate the branch from the vine and it will wither and die. No further fruit will be forthcoming. The branch is so totally dependent upon the vine that the branch is not even aware of producing fruit. It just "shows up." So it is with us.

We find ourselves in the same boat as Jesus. He was unable to heal, raise the dead or cast out demons on His own. He could only do what He saw the Father doing. (John 5:19) We, likewise, are unable to heal, raise the dead or cast out demons on our own power. Think of the analogy in Chapter 2 of the trolley cars and electricity. Jesus reminds us that without Him we can nothing. (John 15:5)

The promise is that if we are abiding in Jesus, He will abide with us. We may ask whatever we wish and it will be done. Remember, the condition is abiding in Jesus, which has a profound effect on what you will ask.

If we are abiding in Jesus we can be certain that He desires to Baptize us with His Holy Spirit. Ask and you will receive.

Don't Ask for Too Little

In the 1960's and 1970's it was most common in our experience for believers to seek Baptism with the Holy Spirit with the target being praying in tongues. When Nancy asked for Baptism with the Holy Spirit she said, "I want to be baptized with the Holy Spirit and pray in tongues." We did not know or understand that there were other pieces to the puzzle. Tongues was the firebrand issue. Tongues was the target.

I pursued tongues after reading *Nine O'clock in the Morning* by Dennis Bennett, an Episcopal priest who was a leader in the charismatic movement. The book may have addressed other issues but the seminal issue for me was tongues.

Since neither of us understood we should expect more, we did not actively seek or request any of the other manifestations of the Holy Spirit enumerated in 1 Corinthians 12:7-10.

I was quite surprised to find that after asking for Baptism with the Holy Spirit I often knew things about people and situations that I had no basis for learning. In fact, it seemed somewhat spooky. I was quite surprised to have a more mature Christian point out that I was receiving words of knowledge.

When you ask for Baptism with the Holy Spirit, you are asking that the Father pour out His Spirit on you. You are not asking for a sprinkling. You are asking to be drenched.

When the Father pours out His Spirit, you can legitimately expect that the Holy Spirit will use you for His purposes, the common good. You should expect the Holy Spirit to manifest through you in all circumstances. The specific manifestation will depend upon the discretion of the Holy Spirit. However, bear in mind that as God finds you trustworthy in little things, He will entrust you with more.

The manifestations of the Holy Spirit do not await your becoming "mature" enough to expect them. The Holy Spirit is already mature. He will be accomplishing His purposes through manifestations of Him, not of you. In my case, I am thrilled to have the manifestation of the Holy Spirit upon me. I find that no one is looking for a manifestation of Jeffie.

Asking the Holy Spirit to manifest Himself through you requires that you surrender to His agenda. The question is not how much of the Holy Spirit you have – you have all of Him – but rather how much of you the Holy Spirit has. As you lay down your agenda and adopt His, you will find more and more manifestations of the Holy Spirit operating in your life.

Not Limited to One "Gift"

Nancy and I often encounter Christians who have been taught that we are given "one gift" with Baptism with the Holy Spirit. These folks ask such things as, "What is your gift." If you believe that you can only receive one "gift" and you have received a private prayer language (tongues), you must feel that the other manifestations listed in 1 Corinthians 12 are not for you. Our experience shows otherwise.

The more liberal of the "one gift" folks tend to admit that, yes, you may get more than one – perhaps two or three. Still, the most common manifestation of the Holy Spirit in their life becomes a limiting influence on their cooperation with the Holy Spirit. "My gift is _____. I can't do that."

The laundry list of manifestations of the Holy Spirit from 1 Corinthians 12 is discussed in the context of the Body of Christ, with all of the parts of the body being necessary. Paul emphasizes that no one part of the body performs all the functions necessary to successful life. The mouth does not both speak and hear. An ear is necessary.

Examination of the actual language of 1 Corinthians 12 quickly dispels the idea that any person may only receive one "gift."

> [7] *Now to each one the manifestation of the Spirit is given for the common good.*

> *[8] To one there is given through the Spirit a message of wisdom, to another a message of knowledge by means of the same Spirit,*
> *[9] to another faith by the same Spirit, to another gifts of healing by that one Spirit,*
> *[10] to another miraculous powers, to another prophecy, to another distinguishing between spirits, to another speaking in different kinds of tongues, and to still another the interpretation of tongues.*
> *[11] All these are the work of one and the same Spirit, and he distributes them to each one, just as he determines.* (1 Corinthians 12:7-11)

The beginning point is that no one is left out. The manifestation of the Holy Spirit is given <u>to each one</u>. This is not a limitation but rather an inclusion.

A second point is that the manifestations are distributed as the Holy Spirit determines. Recall that He is giving these manifestations for the common good, to accomplish His purposes. Accordingly, he often gives a particular manifestation to more than one person in any circumstance to insure that one person who may "sit on" that manifestation does not frustrate His purpose. It is not uncommon for many people in a gathering to receive the same word of knowledge or word of wisdom. It is likewise not unusual for many words of knowledge to be given to many people about the same issue, each word furnishing different shades and phases of the issue. The combination of all the words gives a more complete picture.

The language "to one there is given through the Spirit" is not intended to be language of limitation. Paul does not say the Spirit gives each person only one manifestation. Rather, Paul emphasizes the distribution among the body so that all recognize they are essential to the proper functioning of those gathered at that time.

Finally, on this issue, verse 11 says, "*he distributes them to each one, just as he determines*." This language is quite different from "he distributes one to each person, just as he determines." Any teaching that the Holy Spirit distributes only one manifestation per person is extra-biblical.

CHAPTER NINE

Power from On High

T he Gospel of Luke contains this account of the forthcoming Baptism with the Holy Spirit.

> *⁴⁶ He told them, "This is what is written: The Messiah will suffer and rise from the dead on the third day,*
> *⁴⁷ and **<u>repentance for the forgiveness of sins</u>** will be preached in his name to all nations, beginning at Jerusalem.*
> *⁴⁸ **<u>You are witnesses</u>** of these things.*
> *⁴⁹ I am going to send you what my Father has promised; but stay in the city until you have been clothed with power from on high."* (Luke 24:46-49)

The King James Version states this forecast somewhat differently.

> *⁴⁶ And said unto them, Thus it is written, and thus it behoved Christ to suffer, and to rise from the dead the third day:*

> *47 And that **repentance and remission of sins**
> should be preached in his name among all nations,
> beginning at Jerusalem.*
> *48 And ye are witnesses of these things.*
> *49 And, behold, I send the promise of my Father*
> ***upon you**: but tarry ye in the city of Jerusalem,
> until ye be endued with power from on high.* (Luke
> 24:46-49 KJV) (Emphasis added.)

In each translation, those who would receive the promise of the Father are described as "witnesses of these things." What things? Scripture required that the Messiah (Christ is the same word, different language) would "suffer and rise from the dead on the third day." The Apostles and disciples were about to be witnesses of the multiple trials, beatings, crucifixion, resurrection and ascension of the Messiah. They were being commissioned to tell the story of how the Messiah recovered the keys to the kingdom by the Liar's total defeat. In order to facilitate carrying out that commission, they were to receive the promise of the Father, the outpouring of His Spirit on all men. (Joel 2:28)

When Peter was preaching to the Household of Cornelius, he emphasized several things (Acts 10:39-43):

- We are witnesses of all He did;
- Jesus was killed by hanging on a cross;
- God raised Him from the dead on the third day and caused him to be seen;
- He commanded us to preach to the people;
- All the prophets testify about Him (identifying Him as the Messiah); and
- Everyone who believes in Him receives forgiveness of sins though His name.

Peter was still speaking those words when the Holy Spirit came on all who heard the message. (Acts 10:44)

In Luke's Gospel account, Jesus emphasizes that once the Messiah had risen from the dead the main function the church was to preach His identity as the Messiah (fulfilling the Law and the Prophets), His death and resurrection.

The Church was also to reinforce the message that a new paradigm had been released. The sacrificial doctrines of the Old Testament were no longer relevant. Forgiveness of sins was henceforth predicated on belief in His name.

The witnesses were to begin at home, in their own community (Jerusalem) and then spread the message to the entire world. First "here" and then "there."

A Word of Caution

In the English language, the word "repent" has taken on a meaning nearly unrelated to the Greek word *metanoeo*, translated "repent." Strong's Concordance offers this definition:

> "I repent, change my mind, change the inner man (particularly with reference to acceptance of the will of God)."

The NAS Exhaustive Concordance defines this word as "to change one's mind or purpose."

The English language, influenced in large part by centuries of the Roman Catholic view of sin and repentance, has taken on an additional gloss. The Merriam-Webster dictionary illustrates this additional tone: "to cause to feel regret or contrition, to feel sorrow, regret or contrition for." Another on line dictionary better illustrates the added gloss: "feel or express sincere regret or remorse about one's wrongdoing or sin." It offers as synonyms, "feel remorse, regret, be sorry, rue, reproach oneself, be ashamed."

The problems with this additional gloss are two-fold. First, the liar wants to make sure we run from God and His loving kindness at every opportunity. To accomplish this goal, he emphasizes to us the enormity and repetitive nature of our sins. His goal is self-reproach and shame. We cooperate with him in this task because the Church has reinforced that view of our sin.

The second problem is that this view is unbiblical. Paul deals with repentance directly and contrasts Godly sorrow and worldly sorrow.

> "Godly sorrow brings repentance that leads to salvation and leaves no regret, but worldly sorrow brings death." (2 Colossians 7:10)

Our English language view of "repent" is high on self-reproach and shame while the repentance resulting from Godly sorrow not only leads to salvation but leaves no regret. Godly sorrow results from agreeing with God about the desirability of your conduct. In other words, you arrive at Godly sorrow by changing your way of thinking. This change in your thinking will lead inevitably to a change in your behavior. Most importantly, there is no regret.

Worldly sorrow results from agreement with the enemy. The Liar wants you to believe that, yes, your conduct or thoughts are disgusting. How can a judgmental God forgive you when you keep repeating this abhorrent behavior? Surely you should run and hide from God's presence to escape His wrath – just like Adam and Eve in the Garden.

When viewed properly, repentance wears a smiley face! Crying and a frowning face result from a desire to avoid repentance. However, once you repent, smiles are appropriate because you have salvation and no regret. That is one reason why the Gospel is "good news."

Back to Jesus' Instructions

The NIV translation of Luke 24:47 is "repentance <u>for</u> the forgiveness of sins will be preached in his name to all nations." If this translation is accurate it seems there is a conflict with what Peter told Cornelius' Household. Peter was clear that forgiveness of sins was the result of believing in Jesus. He does not condition forgiveness of sins upon repentance. Peter told Cornelius' Household nothing calculated to create shame or self loathing. Yet, here we have the NIV translators suggesting that "<u>repentance for the forgiveness of sin</u> will be preached in his name to all nations."

The King James Version is entirely different. It renders Luke 24:47 as "repentance <u>and</u> remission of sins will be preached in his name among all nations." A tiny Greek word holds the key to this puzzle.

The Greek word at issue is *kai*. *Kai* is a copulative (or additive) conjunction that is used to connect a word, clause or sentence to an earlier word, phrase or sentence. Does it mean "and" or does it mean "for" or could it be translated properly either way? *Kai* is translated "and" 8,173 times in the KJV. I am unable to find even one instance in which *kai* is translated "for" in the KJV.

In my view, the KJV translation more closely represents the Biblical view of Godly sorrow and repentance stated by Paul in 2 Colossians 7:10. Further, Jesus connected repentance and the good news. "Repent and believe the good news." (Mark 1:15) This is rendered as but one sentence. The implication is clear that repent has to do with a belief system, not a self-judgment system. There is no "good news" in self-loathing and shame.

91

The Second Account

A second account of Jesus' instructions to his disciples is found in Acts 1:5, 8:

> [5] . . . *"[I]n a few days you will be baptized with the Holy Spirit."*
>
> [8] *But you will receive power when the Holy Spirit comes on you; and you will be my witnesses in Jerusalem, and in all Judea and Samaria, and to the ends of the earth."*

This exchange makes it clear that Baptism with the Holy Spirit is to be accompanied by power at the time the Holy Spirit comes <u>on you</u>. Once again, there is emphasis on the function of those receiving this baptism. The recipient becomes equipped to be Jesus' witness, first here at home and then abroad.

The promised power is intended to equip witnesses for Jesus of "these things." The impartation of this power is, primarily, to illustrate how Jesus fulfilled the prophetic scriptures that the Messiah would die, be raised from the dead by God, and ascend to heaven.

Paul's prescription for salvation is:

> *If you declare with your mouth, "Jesus is Lord," and believe in your heart that God raised him from the dead, you will be saved. For it is with your mouth that you profess your faith and are saved. As Scripture says, "Anyone who believes in him will never be put to shame."* (Romans 10: 9-11)

The ability to confess that Jesus is Lord shows a change in your way of thinking (*metanoeo*), an abandonment of your agenda and adoption of His agenda. If you haven't adopted Jesus' agenda, how can He be Lord of your life? Belief in the Messiah requires a belief of resurrection from the dead.

Power to be a Witness

What power does a witness need? A witness recreates through his verbal utterance a truthful account of what happened. Several things are required of a witness.

<u>A witness must know the truth</u>.

I am in my 40th year as a lawyer. Most of my professional life was spent as a trial lawyer, dealing with witnesses. Generally speaking, the first requirement for testimony is a "first hand" knowledge of the facts. Matters of opinion are generally not permitted except from "experts" and those expert opinions are considered only in limited circumstances. Hearsay knowledge of the facts is generally not permitted except in extremely limited circumstances where the circumstances themselves give reliability to the truthfulness of statements of others.

The power to be a witness starts first and foremost with the knowledge of the truth of "these things." Where does that come from when "these things" occurred more than 2000 years ago? Paul provides the answer. *"I keep asking that the God of our Lord Jesus Christ, the glorious Father, may give you the Spirit of wisdom and revelation, so that you may know him better."* (Ephesians 1:17) Revelation knowledge is the most reliable knowledge of the truth. When God's Spirit is poured out on us, we can expect access to revelation knowledge when we need it for the common good.

God's Spirit also brings with Him access to God's wisdom when we need it for the common good. God's wisdom is far superior to ours.

Jesus also addressed knowledge of the truth. *"If you hold to my teaching, you are really my disciples. Then you will know the truth, and the truth will set you free."* (John 8:31) Do not forget that Jesus also said, *"I am the way and the truth and the life. No one comes to the Father except through me."* (John 14:6)

We should expect to receive the power to know the truth of "these things" when God's Spirit is poured out on us.

A witness is permitted to see the Hand of God at work.

Jesus promised "You <u>will be</u> my witnesses." (Acts 1:8) The Greek word *esomai* indicates a future occurrence. Something is going to happen to permit us to be His witnesses.

A witness needs to be present at the "scene of the crime." If I am not there, how can I be a witness? Thus, the power necessary for me to be Jesus' witness is the power to recognize the work of the Hand of God. I need to know when God is working.

What better way to be able to recognize the work of the Hand of God than to be a co-laborer with God. Paul calls us laborers together with God. (1 Corinthians 3:9 KJV) The NIV phrases it as "we are co-workers in God's service." If we are going to adopt Jesus' agenda, we have to discern what the Father is doing. (See John 5:19) When we have discerned what the Father is doing, we can become yoked together with Jesus, whose yoke is easy. Jesus invites us to take His yoke upon us and learn from Him. He promises that we will find rest for our souls, that He is gentle and humble in heart. We need power from on high to experience that Jesus yoke is easy and His burden is light. (Matthew 11:28-30)

<u>A witness tells what he knows to re-create the event</u>.

The purpose of testimony from knowledgeable witnesses is to re-create the event for the judgment of the judge or jury. The witness is not permitted to be either a judge or a juror. Rather the judge and jurors must rely upon the re-creation of the event by those who were there.

Testimony is given for the purpose of eliciting a desired response. A trial lawyer presents those witnesses who evoke the "view" of the event desired. Every trial involves conflicting presentations of the truth as discerned by the witnesses. Unfortunately, I have never been in a trial when the witnesses for both sides have told the same "truth." Thus, one of the jobs of the lawyer is to demonstrate to the fact finder why the version offered from his witnesses is more reliable that the version offered by the opposition.

Life gives rise to conflicting versions of the truth. One of the constants in our life is the presence of the liar offering a different version of reality. The best witnesses are those who can present the truth in a manner that demonstrates the accuracy of his observation while contradicting the liar's version.

One of the characteristics of a good witness is one who "stays hitched." The other side is trained to create doubt from your witnesses and enhance truth from his witnesses. If a witness is uncertain or changes his testimony on cross examination, the witness' reliability is significantly reduced.

The liar does all he can to keep us from "staying hitched." What approach did the liar use in the Garden of Eden? He asked Eve, *"Did God really say, 'You must not eat from any tree in the garden?"* (Genesis 3:1)

First, he approached the resident of the Garden who did not have first hand knowledge. God instructed Adam. Eve heard it from Adam.

Second, he used half-truths. God did indeed say not to eat certain fruit. He did not say not to eat all fruit.

Good witnesses for Jesus will know the truth so as to not become confused and will easily recognize half-truths from the liar.

The liar used a similar approach when tempting Jesus. When Jesus was baptized, upon coming up from the water He heard a voice from heaven saying, "You are my Son, whom I love; with you I am will pleased." (Luke 3:22) He received confirmation directly from heaven that He was God's Son.

One chapter later, the Holy Spirit has led Jesus into the desert where the liar will tempt Him. Two of the three temptations include "If you are the Son of God." (See Luke 4:3, 9) Jesus was not confused that He was the Son of God. His Father in heaven had just told him so. Jesus' certainty in the reliability of this revelation knowledge equipped Jesus to avoid the temptation.

A good witness for Jesus needs to be strong in his knowledge of God's Word (what did God say) and his status (who does God say you are). We should expect the power from on high to be Jesus' witnesses to include the power to learn and rely on God's Word and to discern and rely on our status in the kingdom.

A witness re-creates reality.

When all the testimony has been heard, the reality of the prior situation has been re-created. The fact finder then issues its judgment of what that reality was.

The Revelation of Jesus tells us "the testimony of Jesus is the Spirit of prophecy." (Revelation 19:10) The testimony of Jesus is not limited to Jesus speaking as a witness. Rather, the testimony of Jesus includes testimony of reliable witnesses of and concerning Jesus. The testimony of Jesus is a re-creation of what Jesus did or said, either in remote times or at the present. It is not only what Jesus did then, but also what He has been doing now.

Prophecy is God's word. If it is not God speaking, it is not prophecy. God's spoken word is the most powerful force in the universe. By it, He created everything that was created. Thus, there is a creative power inherent in God's word.

This creative power in God's word can be brought to bear on a particular situation by giving the testimony of Jesus. The testimony of what Jesus is doing currently is an invitation for repetition. The testimony from reliable witnesses becomes the powerful spoken word of God which can and does perform the same now as it did then.

I experienced a creative miracle when God healed the nerves leading to my left deltoid muscles which had been injured in a third surgery on my left shoulder. Not only did He heal the nerves, He later replaced the muscle fiber that had become atrophied over a period of fourteen years.

I have often given this "testimony of Jesus." I am thrilled to be able to do so. In many instances, the mere recitation of this testimony has led to spontaneous, sovereign healing of shoulder injuries in those hearing the testimony. This spontaneous healing includes people who have simply heard the testimony over the Internet. No prayer has been required. The testimony by itself released healing.

Many who have not been healed sovereignly following hearing this testimony have likewise been healed after receiving prayer. The "testimony of Jesus" created an atmosphere in which what happened before was more likely to happen again. Nancy and I have seen this many times.

The power to be Jesus' witnesses includes participation in a release of healing power through a recounting of the testimony of that which Jesus is doing on the earth.

A witness cannot do that to which he testifies.

While it is true that a witness re-creates the prior reality, the witness does not become able to perform the acts to which he testifies. A witness needs no power to lift weights to testify that a weight lifter performed a dead lift of 200 pounds. A witness reports what someone else has done.

A witness who saw Nolan Ryan pitch a baseball 100 miles per hour does not need to be able to pitch at any speed. In spite of the witness' inability to pitch, Nolan Ryan could still throw it 100 miles per hour. The witness never becomes confused about who acted and who reported.

The power from on high to be Jesus' witness does not require any power to perform the act described. The power needed is to accurately observe, report and stay hitched.

A witness needs verbal ability.

The most reliable witness is virtually useless without the ability to communicate what he has witnessed. Sharing "things of God" comes with difficulty to most of us.

Power from on high to equip us to be Jesus' witnesses includes access to the right words at the right time to serve God's purposes. We need not worry about finding the right words. Jesus' instruction was "do not worry about what to say or how to say it. At that time you will be given what to say." (Matthew 10:19; see also Mark 13:11 and Luke 12:11)

Conclusion

We can rest assured that God does not commission us to perform an act without equipping us beforehand for the task. He would never be so mean as to require us to do something without, at the same time, furnishing the ability to not only do it, but do it well.

Baptism with the Holy Spirit includes access to power from on high necessary to work with Jesus while resting in His power and His authority. A large part of Baptism with the Holy Spirit is surrendering yourself to God's purposes so that His agenda ascends to the top of our list.

CHAPTER TEN

A Likely Attack

Once you have received Baptism with the Holy Spirit, the enemy is not going to be happy. His most likely attack against you will be an attempt to have you question your experience. If the liar can convince you that you "didn't get it," then you will set aside this precious gift rather than pursue the matters of God with even greater vigor.

One of the tricks Nancy and I have observed quite regularly is to get the believer to focus on himself and make comparisons to other Christians. You want to know that you got the real goods so you take inventory of what you have perceived so far. You look for the manifestations of the Holy Spirit in your life and compare those manifestations to those others have experienced.

Beware of any theology based on lack. If I have not experienced an interpretation of tongues, the enemy will point that out to suggest that I have not truly experienced the other manifestations listed in 1 Corinthians 12. If he can convince me the utterances that came from my mouth were gibberish rather than tongues, he can tempt me to abandon seeking any of the manifestations of the Holy Spirit.

Jealousy is a strong foe because we feed it so regularly. Nancy and I experience manifestations of God's presence differently. I become electric throughout my body. Nancy has oil and gold dust appear on her hands. We have learned that when I am electric, chances are excellent that she will have oil and gold dust.

Gold dust is flashy. I have wanted it since I first heard about it. While I have in fact experienced it upon occasion, it is not a regular occurrence for me. I am fairly convinced that God does not manifest His presence to me with gold dust because He knows it would make me nearly insufferable.

Feeling electric is not so flashy – unless it is your body that is affected. Feeling electric for me is the usual manifestation of God's presence. It has never happened to Nancy.

I needed to learn that having either gold dust or electricity was not a red badge of courage. Neither signifies greater love or acceptance in the kingdom. Neither is better, they are only different.

If I permit my selfish desire to have gold dust to diminish my awareness of God's presence through the electric feeling, the enemy has gotten a toe-hold. When Nancy and I discuss this matter, she always asks me, "Are you willing to give up feeling electric for gold dust?"

My response illustrates my lack of maturity. I want it all. I not only desire gold dust, I also desire the electric feeling. What's wrong with that, you ask. The problem is that both gold dust and the electric feeling are manifestations of God's presence, not a manifestation of the worthiness of the person on whom He is manifesting. If God is present, He is present. He could not be "more present" with both gold dust and electricity. He is simply, and magnificently, present.

We have learned that God's presence brings with it all His power. He doesn't leave home without it.

I urge you not to become distracted by what you don't have or have not experienced. Show yourself trustworthy in small matters and God will give you greater authority.

About the Author

Jeffrey Thompson retired from the practice of law after forty years' experience, principally as a trial lawyer in complex civil trials. He and his wife, Nancy, live in Leander, Texas, where they can easily dote on their grandchildren.

Jeffrey and Nancy experienced an explosion in their pursuit of supernatural ministry in 2008 that continues to this day. Not only have they experienced substantial favor from God in delivering His compassion to His people, they also have experienced favor in equipping the saints to do the same.

They would love to come to your church or group to conduct a seminar on supernatural ministry. You should expect for the participants in that seminar to experience and participate in miracles, signs and wonders commencing in the first session and continuing the balance of your life.

Contact Information

Jeffrey B. Thompson
2008 Granite Hill Drive
Leander, Texas 78641
817-243-6123
866-720-1316 (fax)
jbt@jbtattorney.com